VOICE OF A SOLDIER:

Operation Liberty
An Anthology of Heroism

Compiled by Margaret Marr

*Betty!
Thanks so much
for everything!
Margaret Marr*

Cover Art by Lori Zecca
*The color picture in the middle of the Cover Art was taken
at Ground Zero in New York City in 2002 by Ms. Zecca.

© Copyright 2006
Sunpiper Media Publishing
ISBN 0-9770050-2-X

DEDICATION:

This book is dedicated to each and every American who has served in any branch of the United States Armed Forces and the families that have loved and supported those brave men and women. Whether serving in combat or enduring the training and preparation to protect this wonderful country in which we live, this book is merely a small token of gratitude earned by each an every one. They are the true American Heroes.

--Greater love hath no man than this, that a man lay down his life for his friends. (John 15:13 KJV)

VOICE OF A SOLDIER:

Operation Liberty
An Anthology of Heroism

Compiled by Margaret Marr

Sunpiper Media Publishing would like to give a special thanks to Margaret Marr, who heard the call of heroes past and answered it with this moving compilation. Thank you for honoring those that defend our freedom.

VOICE OF A SOLDIER

Honors two organizations that directly support America's wounded heroes. Thanks to your purchase of this book, you have supported them as well. Please check out the organizations listed below to find out what more you can do for American service men that have put and continue to put their lives on the line for each and every American.

God bless America and God bless the American Soldier!

www.operationfirstresponse.org

www.woundedwarriors.org

TABLE OF CONTENTS

FOREWORD

Just as the stories revealed on the pages that follow, it is very hard to imagine how one decision can change the course of so many lives. Since the day my child made his decision to join the United States Army, nothing has been the same, my eyes were opened to a world that I never imagined could impact me so powerfully; The realism that our Nation has been built on the strength, courage and blood of our truest source of heroes; *our soldiers, marines, airmen and sailors.*

For the past three years, as the President of Operation First Response, Inc., I have had the honor to serve our wounded and their families. I have been able to witness first hand their strength and devotion. I have walked the halls of Walter Reed Army Medical and felt the presence of heroes. It's impossible to spend five minutes with them without transformed and inspired by their patriotism for our Country and the love they have for their comrades.

Voice of a Soldier gives an accurate portrayal of the many military heroes that have been lost in conflicts throughout our history. The actions discussed were sometimes their last, however, those acts often changed the lives that they left behind forever. Some will be remembered in the tear of a fellow comrade on Veteran's Day and others will have their names carried on by the first-born son of a battle buddy, however, all will be remembered each time our Flag is raised.

As you read each story of valor in, Voice *of a Soldier,* you will begin to realize that these are not just words on paper, but lives that have changed the course of our great Nation. Stories that continuously need to be told: continuously need to be heard and never, ever forgotten.

By Peggy Baker
Voice of a Soldier's mom
President and Co-Founder of Operation First Response
www.operationfirstresponse.org

SAFE IN THE ARMS OF LOVE
BY
MARGARET MARR

Margaret Marr lives in the mountains of western North Carolina where she spends her days working for Shannon Taylor Trucking and her nights for Southwestern Community College.

She's a multi-published author of paranormal novels with romantic elements. Her next release, *Wings of Thunder*, will be available from Publish America in late 2005 or early 2006. Margaret is also a regular contributor to the e-zines *Seven Seas Magazine* & *Nights and Weekends*.

When she's not working her two jobs or writing, she spends time with her two boys. She likes to hike, swim, camp, and fish in the dark. While her boyfriend is away serving in the Air Force, Margaret shares her bed with two mommy cats and five kittens, which like to hog the pillow and blanket when a cold wind is blowing outside.

Visit Margaret Online at: **http://margaretmarr.bravehost.com/index.html**, or drop her an e-mail at: **mizz_scarlett@hotmail.com**.

CPL J.C. Dills US Marine Corps
Somewhere in Vietnam

SAFE IN THE ARMS OF LOVE
By
Margaret Marr

Sleep and dream the
Night away
Hush my quiet fears
Angels in glory
Fly with my beloved
Soldier tonight

Wild imaginings haunt
Endless hours of darkness
Wrapped snug in cotton
Cold without his warmth
Hush now...

All is safe
All is secure

Rest in peaceful repose
Your adored soldier is tucked
In your heart
And nestled in God's hands

A LEGACY OF HEROES – PAST & PRESENT
BY
MARY EMMA ALLEN

Mary Emma Allen writes for many inspirational publications and anthologies. Currently she's working on a children's novel based on her ancestor's experiences during the Civil War era. She grew up during WWII and relates these memories for her daughter and grandchildren so they'll have an appreciation for the men and women who have kept and currently are keeping our country free. Visit Mary Emma at **http://homepage.fcgnetworks.net/jetent/mea**. Email: **me.allen@juno.com**.

...he has been amazed in recent years, when wives and children of other Korean War vets remark, upon meeting him and learning of his work during the war, "you [and others like you] saved my husband's life. You saved my father." Then they thank him ardently.

A LEGACY OF HEROES – PAST & PRESENT
By
Mary Emma Allen

Non-Fiction

Our military men and women, throughout history, have been performing duties that may seem a routine part of their job, even though dangerous at times. They may have wondered what they were doing in that situation, whether defending their country on its own soil or far from home, whether in wars during our history or the present day.

The military personnel, as well as civilians associated with the war endeavor in Iraq often may feel the same way and wonder if what they're doing has any significance. However, in years to come, they'll discover they've influenced the lives of future generations in this country, the Middle East, and the world.

A discussion with a Korean War veteran brought this home recently. At our yard sale, Joe browsed among the tables of books, tools, dishes, and other items. Then he and my husband, a Vietnam War era Air Force pilot, began comparing stories about their military experiences.

Joe, a former paratrooper, had gone behind the lines to rescue men and bring out wounded during the Korean conflict.

"It was just my job," he remarked. "I was just an 18-year old kid and had no thoughts of being a hero."

Scared at times, gaining the tough knowledge of experience, he was doing what he was trained for, although when he enlisted, he had no idea this was in his future.

However, he has been amazed in recent years, when wives and children of other Korean War vets remark, upon meeting him and learning of his work during the war, "You [and others like you] saved my husband's life. You saved my father." Then they thank him ardently.

These wives and adult children further explain that a husband or one who became a husband and father lived because paratroopers like Joe saved his life by bringing him out of a dangerous situation. Sometimes the woman had not known the man who would become her husband when Joe or his buddies rescued him. She knew only that he had lived to marry her because of the paratroopers and pilots and their support teams.

"You fellows are our heroes," one son told him.

The deeds of an 18-year old paratrooper affected the lives of people 50 years later. Their lives were transformed because Joe and others like him served their country and performed the duties for which they were trained without thoughts of being heroes.

I also think of my uncle who served in World War II, another uncle in World War I, uncles who joined the Army in various states

16

during the Civil War, and great, great, great grandfathers who fought for freedom during the Revolutionary War.

They had not realized future generations would learn of their service and be thankful these men were willing to put their lives on the line for their families and freedom. Our military in Iraq, through service and loyalty to their country, also are transforming the world for years to come. They're heroes doing a job, sometimes seemingly a thankless one, which will have an influence upon future generations.

Our heartfelt thanks goes out to the men and women fighting for freedom, sometimes giving their lives, to ensure a safer world and future for all of us.

LOVE BEYOND BRAVE
BY
ANN MARIE BRADLEY

Ann Marie Bradley inherited her love of books and writing from her mother, and her interest in creative writing stretches back to when she was a child. Her favorite type fiction combines her love of cats and the paranormal. These days her stories are far from traditional romances. Each heroine has a pet cat, based on one of the author's own cats.

Ann spins tales of love and intrigue, with heroes to die for. Reality shifts behind dangerous shadows, delves into the past through time travel or reincarnation, and always sweeps you away through the realm of sweet romance and imagination. Ann has won many awards and contests for her writing, and has been published in magazines and newspapers. She is currently working on a novel-length manuscript, FOREVER OVER ALL. She also has a non-fiction short story published in the anthology, LET US NOT FORGET, a tribute to America's 20th century veterans, and has written radio commercials. You can read excerpts of Ann's work on her web site at **http://www.annmariebradley.com**.

SP-4 Jeffrey J. Tracey
Receiving the Bronze Star of Valor for gallantry in action against hostile forces

While young idealists staged violent sit-ins and protests of the war, burned their draft cards, even fled to Canada, Jeffrey marched through hostile Vietnamese villages, dodged land mines, and survived night attacks and enemy raids. He lost his innocence on the battlefield to give those at home in America-the-beautiful the chance to stay free.

LOVE BEYOND BRAVE
By
Ann Marie Bradley

Non-Fiction

In 1966 I was a sophomore in high school. Just like most of my classmates, I worried about basketball scores, the latest pop albums, Mod fashions, who was dating whom, and scooping the loop in my '57 Chevy.

My eighteen-year-old brother-in-law, Jeffrey J. Tracey, had a tad more to worry about. He kissed his new bride of less than a year, my sister, Hazel, goodbye, left her with my parents, and traveled to Fort Knox, Kentucky to endure six weeks of basic training in the United States Army. He mastered guerrilla warfare, including the use of an M-14 rifle, M-60 machine gun, and 3.5-rocket launcher at Fort Polk, Louisiana. Finally he boarded a plane with many other young service men and women headed for Vietnam, ready to fight for freedom and the American way of life.

Proud to be an American, Jeffrey stood up for his flag and country. Sure, he wanted to stay home in this sweet land of liberty with his family; he didn't want to kill, to die. But if not for his and all the other soldiers' sacrifice and patriotism, where would this nation be? While young idealists staged violent sit-ins and protests of the war, burned their draft cards, even fled to Canada, Jeffrey marched through hostile Vietnamese villages, dodged land mines, and survived night attacks and enemy raids. He lost his innocence on the battlefield to give those at home in America-the-beautiful the chance to stay free.

On the home front The Beatles new song, Michelle, hit the pop charts, women burned their bras, and African-Americans fought for equal rights, attracting the media. The burden of fighting trained VietCong guerillas fell to the unsung heroes, the 200,000 American soldiers fighting for what they believed.

While Americans sat in their comfortable living rooms, watching the characters of a new TV show, Star Trek, battle aliens, and Zsa Zsa Gabor battle Batman, our young servicemen faced real death and torture from tough enemy soldiers hiding in the thick forests and rugged hills, ready to inflict horrendous casualties on allied fighting men.

Late one night Jeffrey's company patrolled a strip of rice paddies and scrub-covered hills known to be ambush sites. Without warning, one man stepped into a booby-trap which exploded a grenade. Shrapnel dug into Jeffrey's leg, but he ignored his own pain and assisted the fallen soldier. Not until the severely injured man was flown by helicopter to a hospital ship would Jeffrey accept medical aid. He was awarded the Purple Heart for his wound.

Safe and sound in my hometown, I viewed a long-ended war in the new movie, Doctor Zhivago. Thousands of miles away, the Vietnam War escalated and the battles were never ending. The young, decorated soldier buried his pain in his soul and continued to give his all.

Amid unending rain, the men in the 4th division, exploitation platoon prepared to move out. Not really knowing what to expect, they strapped on their gear and crawled through thick mud and water near Kontum Province. Well-aimed enemy fire threatened their relocation, but they pushed forward, amid severe mortar barrage. One mortar shell landed within a few feet of the command post. With no concern for his own welfare, acting with spirit and courage that far surpassed the call of duty, SP-4 Jeffrey Tracey pounced on the potentially lethal round, covered it with his helmet, then with his own body. Seconds turned to minutes before the men realized the mortar had failed to detonate. Battalion commander, Colonel Duquivm, later decorated Jeffrey with the Bronze Star of Valor for gallantry in action against hostile forces.

Jeffrey pushed himself. His strong faith, along with dreams of Hazel and their unborn child, compelled him until he could return to America. In the combat, he suffered another wound, this time to the shoulder, earning his second Purple Heart.

In October of 1967 Jeffrey came home to his wife and their three-month-old baby girl. However, he hadn't left the horrors of war behind; at times unable to think of all who hadn't come back, including his best buddy, a South Vietnamese soldier named Dang. Although he'd fought honorably, he suffered nightmares, trapped in memories of the battlefields. Still, he'd given his all for what he believed, taken bullets for his country, fought so people could choose their own course with free elections.

Taking glory in his country, his flag, and his service, Jeffrey wore his uniform proudly to march in parades, joined the VFW and American Legion, serving as commander. Each Veteran's and Memorial Day, with trembling hands, he spent hours placing small American flags on the soldiers' graves at the local cemetery.

I was with Jeffrey in November of 1999 as he fought his last battle and lost - the battle with cancer. Towards the end, I gave him a hug and whispered I was proud of him for serving his country. Seems like too little too late.

His family holds loving memories of Jeffrey deep inside. Significantly displayed in his wife's home along with the American flag are Jeffrey's medals - a Purple Heart with one cluster, Combat Infantry Badge, Unit Citation with one cluster, the National Defense Ribbon, Vietnamese Service Ribbon with two clusters, Vietnamese Campaign Ribbon, and the Bronze Star of Valor.

I place my hand upon my heart and salute you, Jeffrey. God bless America. Let freedom ring.

KEEP THE FAITH
BY
STEVEN MANCHESTER

The father of two sons and one beautiful, little girl, Steven Manchester is the published author of *The Unexpected Storm: The Gulf War Legacy, Jacob Evans, A Father's Love, Warp II* and *At The Stroke of Midnight,* as well as several books under the pseudonym, Steven Herberts. His work has been showcased in such national literary journals as *Taproot Literary Review, American Poetry Review* and *Fresh! Literary Magazine.* Steven is an accomplished speaker, and currently teaches the popular workshop "Write A Book, Get Published & Promote Your Work". Three of his screenplays have also been produced as films. When not spending time with his children, writing, teaching, or promoting his published books/films, this Massachusetts author speaks publicly to troubled children through the "Straight Ahead" Program. Visit Steven Online at: **http://www.StevenManchester.com**.

The camp was quiet; everyone tucked in for the night. I looked out into the black desert and picking up my rifle, removed the banana clip, leaving one round in the chamber. Feeling very much alone, I walked into the darkness.

KEEP THE FAITH
By
Steven Manchester

Non-Fiction

In August of 1990, a disturbing headline of the daily Boston Herald read: IRAQ INVADES KUWAIT! I knew then that my life would be changed forever.

Saddam Hussein had invaded Kuwait with his henchmen, compiling the fourth largest army in the world. The atrocities and inhumane acts committed toward Kuwait prompted support from around the globe. War was declared. The world called it Operation Desert Storm and volunteer soldiers were called to serve their countries. Within a few short months, soldiers, sailors, airmen and marines arrived in the Middle East to defend Saudi Arabia, liberate Kuwait and embarrass the biggest bully of the post cold war era. I was one of those soldiers.

The responsibilities brought to bear were immense. There was so much at stake. Politically, there was America's leadership of the free world. Economically, there were one-tenth of the world's oil resources. Morally, there was the protection of human life. But silently, there was a rebirth of America's spirit. The veterans of Operation Desert Storm went to heal their nation from a ghost that had haunted them for two decades—the poltergeist of Vietnam.

Before shipping out, each night I found myself surrounded by family and friends. There was no solitude, though, not one moment of privacy. Everybody needed some time with me. They all hoped for the best, but each one anticipated the worst. Every second seemed precious, but as most felt it could be the last moments spent with me, it was anything but enjoyable. Still, my mask of strength was held firmly in place.

On the night before I was to report to duty, my family threw a party. Almost as if it had been rehearsed, there were apologies for disagreements long forgotten. There were wishes of luck and promises of daily prayers. I repressed every emotion that churned inside of me, but the mood of the room darkened even more and everybody started telling me, "Good-bye": Everyone but my Mom. It was the very reason they had all come: some to clear their consciences, others to relieve their doubts and worries—most just to grieve. I was smothered by hugs and kisses, as they each said their good-byes. It was unbelievable. They were mourning the death of a man they truly loved, a man who was still breathing and with each breath, trying to console them. Sitting in the middle of my own wake, my thoughts spiraled downward. Everything was there but the casket. I looked to my brothers for support, but they were grieving themselves and were now sedated from alcohol. And then my Mom approached me and took me in her arms. "Keep the faith," she whispered. This also upset me, but little did I know, those three simple words would echo in my head for months to follow. It would become a welcome and comforting echo.

As a shield was replaced by an angry storm, Saddam Hussein threatened America with the mother of all battles. In turn, President George Bush drew a line in the sand. That line was quickly wrapped around Iraq and used to choke the life out of thousands.

Though Hussein swore it would take us months to cross the breach from Saudi Arabia to Iraq, it took only hours. We moved fast, crushing the first of three Iraqi lines of defense. As if they weren't even there, we rolled right over them. It was clear: While Hussein chose to sit out the air campaign, the Iraqi people bore the brunt for their ruthless dictator and like all victims of war; they paid with gallons of their own blood. It was literally hell on earth.

History was made. In triumph, Kuwait was liberated, while Hussein was humiliated before the whole world. An unconditional withdrawal was ordered. Politically, the sadistic demon was slain. In reality, unlike thousands of his own people, he still lived.

Although Iraq surrendered, the fighting for many of us was far from over. While America's technology continued to erase the poltergeist of Vietnam, many of us were invaded with their own ghost of torment. Amidst the daily chaos, we experienced the frailties of our own mortality and, unlike CNN's sanitized version of the desert clash, the realization that there is no glory in war. Then, as a lasting memento, most of us were brutally introduced to "The Mystery Illness."

Just before nodding off one night, I picked up a letter sent from my Mom and opened it. Her words, which had brought such happiness in Saudi Arabia, now brought sorrow and pain. I couldn't think about home. In fact, it felt like I hadn't been there, or seen my family in years. It seemed a whole different lifetime. From then on, I decided I wouldn't read any more from home. The letters I would send out would all be written in one day, and then assigned fictitious dates. There was nothing good to report and I needed the distance. Every few days, I mailed one out. My family didn't have to know. It was best that only I knew the truth.

But that cancerous secret quickly ate me alive.

Many full moons had come and gone, while things changed, but only for the worse. There was more death—the death of sinless children. The war had been over for weeks, but as I'd been forced to learn, land mines refused to surrender. My comrades and I tried desperately to save each child, but it was always the same story. The choppers either arrived two minutes too late, or the wounds were just so extensive that the flying

23

medics were never called. It was a losing battle every time.

Personally, my body was consumed with pain. My head constantly pounded, my digestive system was completely out of whack, though it was my mind, which carried the greatest burdens. Never realizing that the chronic problems could have been caused by America's inoculations, Iraq's Scud attacks, or the white, chemical residue which covered everything, I was down, always down and could never seem to pick my spirits back up. I could feel the depression engulf me and though I fought it, my body was just too tired. Every waking moment was spent in a vice of anxiety, or all-out panic. Like clockwork, each night my restless sleep was interrupted by severe panic attacks, or demented, life-like nightmares. I could hear the shrills of grown men, smell the smoldering of human flesh and count the amount of cruel and excruciating deaths which I'd witnessed. Each time, I'd awake and try to find the difference between the hellish dreams and my actual life. The answer was simple. There was no difference. My life was the nightmare. I was merely replaying the torment during my sleep. After weeks of the intense suffering, it was time to stop the pain.

The camp was quiet; everyone tucked in for the night. I looked out into the black desert and picking up my rifle, removed the banana clip, leaving one round in the chamber. Feeling very much alone, I walked into the darkness. Overwhelmed with confusing emotions and boggled thoughts, the months of anguish had finally brought despair. My body, my mind, they had both taken enough. Looking back at the camp, I decided that I'd created enough distance. Collapsing onto the cool sand, I gazed up at a majestic sky. Searching hard, I could not find the beauty. It was then that my tortured eyes released a river of tears. Without restraint, I wept hard. I cried for my life, knowing that I was just minutes from ending it. Closing my eyes, I searched within, but could not find any goodness there either. I was on empty. There was nothing left. With no relief in sight, the present was unbearable and the future held no hope. I cried harder. There seemed to be no other choice and that alone scared me more. As the last tear turned to dust, I opened my eyes and looked back into the starry sky. Then, to my surprise, I remembered my family.

For the first time in a long time I pictured my parents, my brothers and young sisters. I hadn't thought about them. I hadn't considered the devastating consequences of my selfish contemplation. Suddenly, I could hear the faint echo of my mother's gentle voice. "Stevie, Keep the Faith!" I cried uncontrollably, knowing that I had lost my faith. Ashamed, I now knelt on the desert floor, no more than a shell of a man. My spirit had been all but crushed, and then for some unexplained reason hope had arrived. And it hadn't showed up a moment too soon. I couldn't kill myself. I couldn't do that to my family. The love that we shared would not allow it. Unloading my rifle, I tossed the brass bullet into the black void. Regaining some composure, I started back toward camp.

As I walked, I realized that my Mom had saved my life. She would never know, nor had she been there in person. It was the strength of her spirit that had awakened my lost soul. I could feel her comfort. Looking inward, I thanked her for sticking by me. Then looking upward, I thanked God. My Mom had given me life, and then without ever realizing it—she'd saved it. Her faith had been strong enough for us both.

Reaching camp, I looked back and could feel my hair stand on end. The moon had cast the softest, most angelic light, illuminating a perfect set of footprints in the sand. Thinking of my Mom, I noticed only one set, though in the deepest part of my broken heart, I knew that I had not traveled alone. My Mom had been right and the truth of it gave me chills. With the effortless strength of a child, I believed. I was not alone, nor did I ever have to feel alone again. The experience would change my life forever. Though everything inside of me would spin out of control, or drift along in great turmoil for many months after, I had been given another chance. I silently vowed to make the most of it.

For the rest of that fateful night, I read two months of unopened letters. I longed to be with my family. I desperately needed them in my life. Their words were encouraging, comforting and overflowing with love. No matter how much it hurt, I would never cast their words aside again. As the sun played peek-a-boo with the sleeping desert, I finished the last letter. Folding it back up, I smiled. It was a last reminder from my Mom; a letter that I should have read weeks earlier. From then on, her advice would not be taken lightly. "I understand now, Mom," I whispered, "I'll keep the faith."

PRISONER OF MEMORIES
BY
ELIZABETH CLEMENTS

As to his God he madly shrieks,
"For this does man exist?"

PRISONER OF MEMORIES
By
Elizabeth Clements

November 11, 1983

The old man snoozes in his chair,
The fire warms his feet,
His peaceful face shows lines of care
And flushes from the heat.

He shivers slightly as he nods
In dreams of long ago,
Where blindly in white hell he plods
Through crusted drifts of snow.

His lashes cling from frozen tears,
He cannot feel his feet,
His shoulders hunch with deathly fears,
His nostrils smell defeat.

The air resounds with laboured breath
And distant battle guns,
And thickens with the stench of death
Of old and young brave sons.

A high pitched whine assaults his ears,
He sees ten soldiers fall,
And over the ridge the foe appears-
They look so fierce and tall.

He hears his leader yell commands
And screams his battle cry,
Then lifts his rifle in his hands
And lands the bullets fly.

The soldiers struggle in the snow
With awful butchery,
And from their wounds the blood does flow-
They shriek their misery.

The snow churns red with spattered blood,
The air splits with their cries,
That stream in one unending flood
Then slowly ebbs and dies.

A stillness spreads across the waste
Of dead and broken men
Who loved to sing and drink and taste
And pampered every yen.

But wait! What is that painful sound
That whimpers in the air?
Oh, there! Beneath a human mound
Stirs one with blood-soaked hair.

He inches from beneath the pile
Of soldiers from his corps;
His throat constricts with bitter bile
At all this senseless gore.

Fresh tears freeze on his blood-smeared cheeks
While shaking mangled fist,
As to his God he madly shrieks,
"For this does man exist?"

And so he stumbles across the miles
Of ravaged, war-torn land,
Which holds no friends nor loving smiles
Nor lends a helping hand.

He staggers in a fevered haze
Of pain and hungriness,
And craves for food through endless days
Which fear cannot suppress.

From broken twigs he eats the leaves
And chews the stringy bark,
And for his home he mutely grieves
While shivering in the dark.

She finds him there that frigid morn,
All hunched in tattered clothes,
So cold and gaunt and face forlorn-
To die is what he chose.

She guides him back to robust health,
Her hands give gentle care;
With him she shares her meager wealth
And soothes his deep despair.

At times she hides him in the woods
When soldiers prowl too near;
They rob her of her precious goods
Of cheese and bread so dear.

In helpless rage he shakes his fist
At their retreating backs;
With deadly calm, he does insist,
"We'll fear no more ransacks."

In moon-less dark they creep away
To seek a better life
And hear the war was won that day,
Which ends their fear and strife.

A chaplain blesses every vow
As Keith and Belle are wed;
A homebound ship he finds somehow,
To Canada it led.

And there they raise four healthy sons
But lose them one by one,
To senseless death by hostile guns
In 1941.

The pain of loss will never leave
The ones who lived the war,
Forever more their hearts will grieve
At life's uneven score.

And as he wakes one gnarled hand kneads
Where bullets ripped raw pain,
And on his brow the cold sweat beads
Like tears of death-chilled rain.

A prisoner of his memories
That haunt his twilight years,
His mind relives grim agonies
Of pain and death and fears.

His little woman bustles in
And hugs her sad-eyed Keith,
"Come, Cherie, they'll soon begin
To pray and lay the wreath."

He stoops before the cross so white
And lays red poppies, slow,
But in his mind he sees a sight
Of blood against the snow.

A small tear slips for all the men
Who died for Liberty,
That gift of hope, for God's children
They gave so we'd be free.

He looks about the silent crowd
That shivers in the cold,
And in his heart he feels so proud
Of comrades brave and bold.

PORTRAIT OF A SOLDIER
BY
JUDE MORRIS

Jude Morris is the mother of Captain Billie Cartwright and the niece of Canadian army veteran Bill Shipton (deceased). As a native Canadian who immigrated to the US in the late 50's, Jude is the author of the Indian Creek Texas mysteries *Deadly Secrets* and *Deadly Betrayal*, and the managing director of the online authors group *Books We Love:* **http://www.bookswelove.net**.

**Captain Billie Cartwright with members of her Unit
and Arnold Schwarzenegger in Bosnia**

"Fill 'er up lads," he said. *"Whatever we've got to spare and don't stint the bacon and eggs. I've a debt to repay and I'll be thanking you not to make me look bad."*

PORTRAIT OF A SOLDIER
By
Jude Morris

Captain Billie Cartwright, a dedicated athlete and inquisitive scientist started life as a premature baby with a tenuous hold on life, but it didn't take her family long to realize that they had a dynamo on their hands. Boundless energy and prickly independence quickly became Billie's hallmarks, and no one was at all surprised to see her follow the footsteps of Grandpa Shipton, her much loved Uncle and substitute grandfather, into military service. Grandpa Shipton loved to entertain his grandkids with wartime tales, and one of Billie's favorites was published by her mom in *Western People Magazine's* Veteran's Day edition.

Western People Magazine, Jude Morris
May, 1991 Egg on His Face

Bill Shipton

Bill was in his glory. Finally after weeks of courting young Phyllis Quelch, he'd been invited home to dinner. He pressed his uniform until the creases cut and shined his shoes until he could see his reflection.

Bill wanted to be sure that the Quelches recognized him as a serious young man with his own land and big plans for the future. Once the war was over he'd be returning to his homestead in Alberta, and it was going to take some doing to convince Phyllis to give up her life in England for the rough Canadian prairies. This dinner was Bill's chance to win the Quelches approval, and when he met them at their humble cottage he flashed his brightest smile and prepared to charm them with his native Canadian wit. The Quelches were a pleasant couple slightly reserved in the manner of the British but they soon warmed to Bill and after dinner they invited he and Phyllis to join them at the neighborhood pub.

32

The evening passed in easy camaraderie. Bill entertained the Quelches with amusing tales of life on the Canadian wilderness, and they responded with anecdotes of English country life. By the time they started home it was raining heavily, and Mrs. Quelch insisted that it was not a fit night for Bill to bicycle back to the base. He gratefully accepted a bed on the living room sofa and was soon fast asleep.

Rising early the next morning to the smell of sizzling bacon, Bill slipped into the little kitchen to greet Mrs. Quelch.

"The top o'the mornin to ya," he quipped. "When I heard you humming away at that stove I thought for a sec I was back home with my Mum."

Smiling shyly, Mrs. Quelch poured him a cup of tea, dished up several slices of bacon and four eggs onto an old crockery plate and set it carefully on the warmer.

"That smells mighty good, ma'am," Bill said, gratefully carrying the plate to the little breakfast nook and happily digging into his breakfast. The portion was just right for his vigorous appetite, and pleasantly filled, he waited eagerly for Phyllis and her Dad to join them. When they finally gathered around the table, Bill wondered that all they ate was toast and tea, but assumed they'd adopted the modern habit of saving their appetite for the mid-day meal.

When Bill prepared to leave for the base Phyllis offered to ride part way and Bill delightedly accepted her company. They hadn't gone far though, when she stopped her bicycle and turned to him with a serious expression on her face. "Bill," she said. "Have you any idea what you've done this morning?"

"Done, why I haven't done anything at all, other than pass the time of day with your Mum and enjoy her fine breakfast."

"That's just it. You ate the entire family's ration of bacon and eggs this morning. We save our eggs all week long so on Sunday morning's we'll have enough to share at breakfast."

Well, the ground should have opened up and swallowed Bill. Never had a young man been so embarrassed. Back home in Canada—what with their own hogs and chickens—it was nothing to eat a rasher of bacon and six or seven eggs for breakfast. It hadn't even occurred to him that the plate Mrs. Quelch put on the warmer was for anyone but himself.

Bill's face flamed. He mumbled his apologies to Phyllis, bid her good day, and pedaled like a madman to the base. Wheeling in through the gates he headed straight for the mess hall. Bill had long been in the habit of offering a helping hand in the kitchen when no one else was willing, and his easy acceptance of even the meanest chores made him a favorite among the cooks. Therefore, when he reached the mess hall and tossed his knapsack in the door he was met with good-natured grins.

"Fill 'er up lads," he said. "Whatever we've got to spare and don't

33

stint the bacon and eggs. I've a debt to repay and I'll be thanking you not to make me look bad."

Next, Bill charged across the compound and descended on the warrant officer. "Sir, every month we're entitled to our ration books." he told the startled officer, "and in all these many months I've not drawn any of mine. This morning I made a colossal donkey of me, what with not knowing how hard-up these people are for food, and I'm sure in need of my ration books."

"Well soldier," the officer replied, "you're certainly entitled to them, but it'll probably take a little time for me to round them up."

"That'll be fine Sir. I've a few things to attend to and then I'll be back to pick them up."

With that Bill headed back to the kitchen, and finding the knapsack filled to overflowing, he thanked the cooks and swung the heavy knapsack onto his shoulders.

When the ration books were ready, he shoved them in his pockets, and fetched his bicycle. Then he pedaled furiously for Maidenhead and was soon knocking on the door of the cottage.

"Why Bill," Mrs. Quelch said, when she answered the door. "Whatever brings you back here this morning?"

"There's a little matter I need to attend to," Bill said stepping inside the door and heading for the kitchen. "You know ma'am," he said, removing the knapsack from his shoulder. "I've never been so embarrassed in my life as when Phyllis told me I'd eaten the family's breakfast. Now, I'm hoping you'll let me makes amends."

Stunned, Mrs. Quelch's eyes widened in wonder as Bill began spilling the contents of his knapsack across the kitchen table. Then, turning to the astonished woman he reached in his pockets and pulled out the stack of ration books.

"Mrs. Quelch," he said. "I want you to know that as long as I'm around here there won't be any more breakfasts of dry toast and tea," and Phyllis, coming into the kitchen, watched in amazement as her mother burst into tears.

"You know," she told Bill later, "in 21 years I've never seen my mum cry, and I'll never forget what you've done for her today."

* * *

Billie possesses a full share of the determination and willingness to do whatever it takes to make things right, that Bill Shipton showed in that English kitchen. From the time of her premature birth in Phoenix, Arizona, Billie's been fighting long odds. Her dad, an American GI in the Korean War, died before Billie's second birthday, and after a five year "settling" period on Shipton's Alberta homestead, Billie's mom, a writer and inveterate gypsy, loaded her girls into the family van and headed back to California. Ten years and five states later, 17-year-old Billie enlisted in the Army and prepared to follow her dreams. After five years of service in Germany, Billie returned to the US with a two-year degree from the American University in Europe, switched to the status of Army Reservist and enrolled at Penn State University to begin studying for her Bachelor of Science Degree in Biochemistry. Interviewed by Army Reservist Magazine in the spring of 2002, Billie explained her philosophy:

I chose this path because it sounded hard and I wanted to see how well I could do. It reflected my own philosophy of life—to take on a challenge head on and apply myself to it wholeheartedly. While I recognize that my goals are high, I don't think they are out of reach and I don't believe you accomplish much if you never take a risk. I also think it is important to verbalize your goals because it makes you accountable.

While at Penn State Billie played an active part in reservist activities, and poor attendance at a Veteran's Day memorial, inspired her to write this article for the campus newspaper:

Where Were You?
Billie Cartwright, member-PSUVO Penn State Press

Saturday, November 11, I was on the steps of Old Main in honor of the veterans who have served our country. As I looked around at the small crowd of people who had assembled, I remembered the enormous group of students, faculty, and administrators who had assembled for the rally on Friday.

This rally took place in response to swastikas being placed around campus along with other forms of intimidation and intolerance. I was at this rally because I abhor these acts. However I am also aware that this is the 50th anniversary of Word War II. The very symbol that generated so much outrage in so many could easily be part of our flag were it not for the soldiers who served. I am sure all of you know at least one veteran, a fellow student, friend, brother, sister, parent, or maybe it is you who is a veteran. Veterans are soldiers—like my dad and my Grandpa Shipton—men and women who served, fought and often died for the very ideals you rallied for. These men and women are the ones who have made it possible for you to demand tolerance. They fought and continue to fight for your freedoms.

Saturday morning there were no classes to walk out of, no chemistry lectures to miss, the mail didn't come, and the banks were closed. I can't believe that all of you were too busy to attend. Did you not recognize the parallel between the rally and the Veterans Day ceremony? One was for peace and the other for honoring those who died for it. On Veterans Day, whom should we honor? All of us lead busy lives and tend to get wrapped up in our own secure little world, still I must ask. ... Where Were You?

* * *

Even a car accident that would have sidelined most people, failed to keep Billie from pursuing her goals and taking the risks inherent in the pursuit:

Everything she hoped for could have ended with a car accident. In May 1999, Army Reserve Capt. (then 1st Lieutenant) Billie Cartwright of the Fort Lewis-based 448th Civil Affairs Battalion nearly brought a promising career that included membership on the All-Army Cross Country Team and running in the Army 10 miler in Washington D.C. to an end after sustaining a fracture in her back. Still, her will to win and her own undaunted determination brought her where she is today...once again competing in her primary sport of distance running and having the opportunity to train with top athletes and run in top notch events. Army Reservist Magazine

* * *

It was characteristic of Billie's indomitable will and her sense of duty that when world events called for more she immediately re-activated to a unit destined for service in Afghanistan, where she emerged as one of the key players in Bamiyan Province.

Afgha - Afghanistan News English Version, 16 May, 2003
© Copyright 1998-2004 Afgha.com

CAT-A projects in Bamiyan are headed by a woman, the aforementioned U.S. Army Captain Billie Cartwright of the 450th Civil Affairs Battalion.

Reconstruction of a country devastated by more than two decades of conflict with extensive involvement by a belligerent seems counter-intuitive. However, the US Military and its Coalition partners have undertaken to assist in doing just that with an alternative reconstruction model combining both security and reconstruction termed the Provisional Reconstruction Team (PRT).

...According to Capt. Billie Cartwright head of CAT-A projects in Bamiyan, one of the gratifying aspects of working in that particular district, is that the residents are overwhelmingly pro-American, which makes working there easier for the team. ...

... Female Inclusion. Another civilian concern was that a predominance of male soldiers would obscure and overlook women's issues. However, an effort has been made to include women in the PRTs:

CAT-A projects in Bamiyan are headed by a woman, the aforementioned U.S. Army Captain Billie Cartwright of the 450th Civil Affairs Battalion.

Captain Billie Cartwright building a road in Afghanistan

* * *

Now back from Afghanistan, and enrolled in the Physician's Assistant program at Duke University, Captain Cartwright continues her reserve duty status with the 450th, while completing the arduous program. Asked about her plans for the future, Cartwright says, "My plans are to work with people in tough situations, slums and poor reservations, places where a physician's assistant is challenged to the limit. I've been fortunate enough to receive full support from the National Health Service Corps through their scholarship service and I will fulfill my obligations in underserved medical areas where I planned to work anyway. As for future military assignments, that remains to be seen."

ANGEL
BY
MARGARET MARR

Margaret Marr lives in the mountains of western North Carolina where she spends her days working for Shannon Taylor Trucking and her nights for Southwestern Community College.

She's a multi-published author of paranormal novels with romantic elements. Her next release, *Wings of Thunder*, will be available from Publish America in late 2005 or early 2006. Margaret is also a regular contributor to the e-zines *Seven Seas Magazine* & *Nights and Weekends*.

When she's not working her two jobs or writing, she spends time with her two boys. She likes to hike, swim, camp, and fish in the dark. While her boyfriend is away serving in the Air Force, Margaret shares her bed with two mommy cats and five kittens, which like to hog the pillow and blanket when a cold wind is blowing outside.

Visit Margaret Online at:

http://margaretmarr.bravehost.com/index.html, or drop her an e-mail at: **mizz_scarlett@hotmail.com**.

JC "Cecil" Dills, CPL US Marine Corp - left
Jewel Vaughn "JV" Dills, SP-4 US Army - right

Cecil Cain lay against the stack of pillows behind his head, his cheeks sunken and his eyes hollow. His death mortgage was almost paid, and it was only a few short hours until the deal was sealed and he received the keys to his mansion in Heaven.

ANGEL
By Margaret Marr
Fiction

In memory of my Uncles:
JC "Cecil Dills", CPL US Marine Corps, Vietnam
(March 18, 1945-May 27, 1991)
Jewel Vaughn "JV", SP-4 US Army, Vietnam
(August 29, 1943-November 6, 2000)

Angel Cain walked down the quiet halls of the Asheville VA Medical Center in North Carolina. Her footsteps echoed off the walls even as her memories echoed through the years: the rat-a-tat tat of machine gun fire, the smell of smoke and stench of burning flesh. Memories of the Vietnam War. Memories she <u>shouldn't</u> have. She was born during the war. How could she remember it?

When she entered the waiting room, JV Ross rose to greet her. "I'm so glad you came." He hugged her, and she felt the cold press of a metal picture frame through her thin blouse.

She pulled back. "How is he?"

JV rubbed his white hair with one wrinkled hand and shook his head. "It won't be long." The Adam's apple in his throat bobbed as he swallowed his pain.

Angel blinked rapidly and looked away. She hated to cry in front of people. But no matter how hard she tried, she could never keep it in check. Especially when she was on stage and a song she sang moved the crowd to tears. She'd end up crying along with them, too choked up to finish the song.

To distract herself, she took the picture from JV's hand. "Who's this?" Her gaze roamed over the black and white photo.

"A picture of me, your Uncle Cecil, and Harris Lindberg."

Three men smiled up at her. They all looked so handsome with their close-cut hair and starched uniforms. Their skin was smooth and untouched by age. Young comrades. "You must've been the best of friends."

"It was hard losing Lindberg to the war, but the night of his death was one night I'll never forget." He paused as if uncertain about saying more. "It's the reason your name is Angel."

She frowned in curiosity. "What do you mean?"

"I can't tell you. Cecil wanted to do it before he passed on. He didn't want to take the secret to his grave."

JV walked her down to her uncle's room, and then left her alone with him. Cecil Cain lay against the stack of pillows behind his head, his cheeks sunken and his eyes hollow. His death mortgage was almost paid, and it was only a few short hours until the deal was sealed and he received the keys to his mansion in Heaven.

Angel believed this with all her heart. She'd often dreamt of Heaven, the dreams so vivid she could almost believe she'd been there once.

Cecil's frail hand groped across the bedspread until he found hers and gripped it weakly. "Sit down, Angel. I've something to tell you."

"Can I get you some water?" She reached for the white Styrofoam pitcher on the table beside his bed, tears threatening to take over again. She loved her uncle so much. He'd been there when her father hadn't.

"No." He gazed out the open window. A gentle breeze blew through the room, ruffling across their skin. Angel knew Cecil loved the feel of the wind on his face. It felt like freedom to him.

Cecil started his story.

"Our platoon left Cu Chi a few days before the Christmas of 1967. Where we ended up on Christmas Day, God only knows. The night was peaceful and calm. A few stars were splattered across a navy blue sky. Sniper fire had been heard in the area, and we stopped to check it out.

"We knelt by the side of the road, waiting. Lindberg chewed on a toothpick, staring off into the trees; JV gripped his M-60 as if afraid it'd be jerked out of his hands by an unseen force; and I stared straight ahead, expecting the unexpected. I had a bad feeling in my gut. Tonight one of us would die.

"Heavy mortar fire exploded fifty yards to the left of me, dirt flew up along with the bodies it'd hit. We quickly took cover and returned fire. The night lit up, not with Christmas lights, but with artillery, ear-splitting explosions and the screams of the wounded and dying.

"We fought for hours without sleep or food. The Vietcong just kept coming at us. I was exhausted and numb. I needed rest. I needed peace. I needed quiet, if only for a few precious minutes. That wasn't what I received. At least not right away.

"At first, I didn't know what caused Lindberg to stand up, run out in the open, shouting and spraying machine gun fire everywhere. I thought I heard him yell, "Don't you dare hurt her!" Bullets shredded his body before I could reach him, knock him down, and drag him back to safety. I watched in horror as his life flowed from him in the form of blood. All I could think was, why Christmas Day? It's a horrible day to die.

"I heard JV cry, "Oh, no, man, not Lindberg. Why did it have to be Lindberg?" I was half afraid JV would go nuts next and get himself killed.

"Suddenly the night was filled with the sweetest voice. The song rose above the line of fire. The words silenced the battlefield. I glanced through the smoke as it cleared and saw a woman in a long white dress, cinched at the waist by a golden rope. She stood at the edge of the trees halfway between the enemy and us.

"She sang, "What Child is This?" and the words echoed between us. Divine words that sank into a man's soul. Her arms spread wide while she sang as if God himself was listening. And I bet He was."

Cecil stopped, rolled his neck on the pillow and looked at her. "She had your face, Angel." His voice wavered. "It was you."

Angel put a trembling hand to her mouth. It all made sense now...the dreams of Heaven, the memories of war, the gift of music, and her birthday...December 25, 1967. Somehow, she'd been sent as an angel on the night of her birth to bring her uncle a small window of peace to renew his strength and his will to keep fighting.

"For one moment in time, the ugliness of a war-torn battlefield was made beautiful." Cecil's eyes drooped shut. "I thank you." They fluttered open and he smiled toward the foot of the bed. "Lindberg thanks you too...he said it was a beautiful night to die..." Cecil closed his eyes for the last time with a smile on his face.

Tears spilled down Angel's cheeks. "You're welcome, Uncle Cecil." She glanced toward the end of the bed. "You too, Harris."

THE SCRAPBOOK
BY
CHRIS POERSCH

Chris Poersch and her husband have lived on his family's fifth-generation farm in northeast Kansas for 32 years. She was ready to stay in one spot, after growing up in a military/ministerial family, and loves the country life. They have three sons, three grandsons and will have two more grandbabies in the spring.

Master Sergeant Jim Godbey
USAF 1945

In my mind, I can still see and feel the rough olive drab material of his fatigues. I sat on their bed watching, pretending to be invisible, thinking that I could maybe squeeze myself into a spot inside the duffel bag and go with him.

THE SCRAPBOOK
By
Chris Poersch

Non-Fiction

It is an old ragged looking thing, dog-eared and fuzzy. The strings holding it together are frayed and are not tied in a bow anymore, just a knot. I'm a little afraid to open the cover to look at the pages for fear that it will crumble apart and I won't be able to gather the crumbs back together into a scrapbook. The color hasn't changed in the almost fifty years since my father gave it to me. It is still a chamois tan, velvety soft, comforting color. It still has the embossed design of an Eskimo girl and her Eskimo father standing in front of the rays of the aurora borealis on the front. The words "Scraps" and "Alaska" are bordered by totem poles framing the little family. It must have taken him weeks to put the scrapbook together during the long dark days and nights while he was stationed in Alaska. Softly and carefully my hand plays over the embossing, the memories flooding back to when he gave this treasure to me. It was during the Korean War that he went several times to Alaska on what was called "TDY" and it was there that he made the scrapbook.

I don't know how many times he went to Alaska during the war and the years after. I remember that he was gone many times but I was very young and a child's memory is a tricky one. I was only partly aware of the sacrifice that he and my mother made when he was away for extended duty. I do remember the preparations for leaving, however. The signs that he had orders to leave were always the same. Papers shown to my mother, quiet talk when we children weren't supposed to be listening, and her tears.

While he packed, I remember the soft jingle his dog tags made as they moved over the beads of the chain. In my mind, I can still see and feel the rough olive drab material of his fatigues. I sat on their bed watching, pretending to be invisible, thinking that I could maybe squeeze myself into a spot inside the duffel bag and go with him. My mother washed and ironed as he precisely folded and tightly rolled most of the clothing. It was all packed into the bag and once the big hook snapped over the folded top, he was finished and ready to go. I know that my mother had to have been aching for him to be done with this part of the ritual of leaving so they could have time alone but before that could happen, we children had our time with him.

Before bed, we piled around him and onto his lap and listened to him spin another Brer Rabbit tale in his soft West Virginian voice. My goodness that was one bad rabbit! Then he told us a Bible story and talked to us about the time that he would be gone and how we were to mind our mama and help her with the chores. He told us that it wouldn't be long and he would be back home. Each of us was hugged and kissed and not one of us was afraid to send him away, even knowing he would be gone long before we awoke in the morning. This was just a part of our military life and, since he always came back, I was not afraid. In all the years growing up, I don't remember ever being afraid because he took care of us and, if he was worried about what was facing him, he kept it to himself. I remember falling asleep listening to the sounds of the planes taking off and flying overhead and hearing my parents' subdued murmurs drifting from their bedroom late into the night. In the morning, he would be long gone by the time we were up to begin the weeks and months of getting used to him being away. I knew that my mother was sad and I had some understanding that my father was the only one who could comfort and reassure her as she prepared to be the single parent, again. It was the life she had accepted in order to be with him. She knew there would be times of separation but she held onto the joy of reunion and there were friends, wives of other Airmen who were also gone from home on duty.

And then, one day, our mother would begin to get ready because he was coming home. We cleaned the house from top to bottom and she made sure to have groceries stocked. She began to get herself ready. She always had her hair done at a salon the day before his return. She carefully put on her make-up and the thing I remember the most was that she could put on red lipstick without even looking in a mirror, a feat I still admire! The last item was the string of pearls he had given her. They were worn for all special occasions, especially for him.

It was the year 1955 when he brought me the scrapbook. We drove to the base to pick him up, right down to where the planes were parked. I remember the sight of him standing in front of an airplane hanger with another Airman. His duffel bag was leaned up against the corrugated tin of the building. When he saw the car, he dropped his cigarette, touched it with the toe of his boot, slung the bag over his shoulder and hurried forward to meet us. My mother stopped the car and ran to him. He let the duffel bag drop to the pavement and grabbed her into his arms. We children were right behind her, yelling and screaming for joy. It wasn't until we got home to our little house on base housing and he began to unpack, handing out the presents he had made for each of us that we calmed down and he and mother could talk. My brothers got totem poles, carved from pieces of pine a foot long. My mother got a hand-tooled leather purse and I was given the scrapbook.

Now, I carefully open the cover of the scrapbook to read the first page, handwritten to me. It says, "For my little girl – Christine - who I love very much. May all things in her life be as beautiful as the flowers above and in the following pages. Remember me when you look at this book." Taped to the page right above the writing is a small pressed flower from the "Tanana Valley, near Fairbanks". There are many dried pressed flowers on following pages, as well as postcards with scenes of Alaska. Scattered throughout are snapshots of him posing in front of planes and with friends. He's wearing a hooded coat "to keep off the mosquitoes", it says under the picture. Another photo is a side view of his face, with a snow-covered mountain behind him. Under it, he wrote, "You have to look quick to see the mountain top because clouds cover the peak most of the time." There is a beautiful sunset picture postcard at the end of the book. Under it, he wrote, "I'm here, you are there and I will always love you no matter how far apart we are."

Oh, Daddy. I do think of you when I see a sunset. If I hear anything about Alaska or see an airplane I think of you. I wish you were here to tell my little ones a Brer Rabbit story. I run my hand over the soft-flocked cover of the scrapbook and remember the feel of your short fuzzy military haircut and the stiffly starched fatigues you wore nearly every day. I sniff the old musty paper pages and think of the smelly, heavy canvas duffle bag, stuffed with the things you had to tightly fit in to take with you when you left before dawn. I let the frayed laces flow through my fingers and remember the dog tags and chain that you had to wear, that were a part of you, a man who lived his whole life in service. Thank you for that. Thank you for the scrapbook. I think I will sit and show my grandsons this book and tell them about the man who pressed flowers and wrote the love notes to his little girl, their Grandma.

My father was stationed at Forbes Air Force Base in Topeka, Kansas, during the fifties and sixties, retiring as a Master Sergeant. He had joined the Army Air Corps in 1942, before he finished high school when he was barely eighteen years old. He served during WWII in North Africa, Normandy and Belgium and he kept the memories of his time there between himself and my mother.

He shared only a few things about WWII with us children. There was a billfold he had made while in Casablanca, a dollar bill with the names of the places he had been written around the edges in a tiny script. There was a small leather photo album with brownish, scalloped-edged snapshots of places and people we didn't know except for one. It was the picture of a lovely young girl in a bathing suit, my mother. It was also the only picture worn and tattered on the corners. And, from there, he brought us our names. My three brothers were named after his buddies Douglas Benson, George Alan and Michael James. My sister and I were named after two little girls, a doctor's daughters, Joycelyn Marie and Christine Aunette, who lived near Antwerp, Belgium.

We are all grown, now, with children and grandchildren of our own. I have been thinking of how to tell my grandsons about my father, whom they never knew. My father got his GED while in the Air Force, retired from the Air Force in 1958 and then went to college and theological seminary, all while raising a family. He served as a pastor in the Methodist Church for twenty-five years. Many times through his life he made comments about how there was too much pain in this world and he just wanted to help heal people's hearts and to be a help to someone who was down. He died on July 10, 1993 and at his funeral the church was so full of old friends he had loved and people he had served that many had to stand at the sides. After the funeral, my mother gave me the service flag that draped his coffin and I keep the tri-folded flag safe, stored with the scrapbook.

BLUE STAR MEMORIAL HIGHWAY
BY
BETTE MILLESON JAMES

Bette Milleson James, a niece/sister/cousin of many family veterans, is a Kansas writer and award-winning teacher of English language arts and technology. She served her school district as grant writer and later wrote original poetry and did research on classic writers for artist N.A. Noel's book, *I Am Wherever You Are.* She also has publication credits in two anthologies, *Let Us Not Forget*, from iUniverse, and *Forget Me Knots...From the Front Porch*, published by Obadiah Press. She and her husband raised three children on a wheat, corn, and livestock farm west of Hoxie Kansas, where they still live, and where she writes daily.

Now at century's end, in momentary peace and safety,
We honor you and all your lost friends,

BLUE STAR MEMORIAL HIGHWAY
By Bette Milleson James
A Tribute to Twentieth-Century Armed Forces

In the first great war of this century,
You fought both men and mustard gas,
Both battles, hand-to-hand, and loneliness, heart-to-heart.
We honored you when you died in the forests of Argonne
For believing with us in the War to End All Wars.

Another great war, and we loved you, our men of the sea,
Whose death came from the air over Pearl Harbor,
And your brothers who died in the skies over Iwo Jima
Or in the mud of Guadalcanal.
We honored American men and American boys too young,
As London burned and Europe bled.
You were our heroes when you stormed the beach at Normandy
And died there, or were maimed, or came back whole.

Korea: We called it "police action," a small war
Full of large death and deep pain.
On ships and planes you went again to a strange land,
Asian and alien, until not a victory but a line was formed:
The thirty-eighth parallel, to end a conflict, to send you home.

Another generation, another war, and thousands more of losses.
There were those who honored you in Southeast Asia,
And there were those who never knew your devotion to duty, to country,
To a long war they neither understood nor believed in.
Reviled on returning, you went again to the same lost war: Vietnam.
In sorrow for a waning pride, you died in faraway jungles,
Or came home changed forever.

Late in the century, a Gulf War, brief, violent, technological:
"Smart bombs" to seek strategic places:
The dangers were different for you here,
But no less deadly. You fought our modern war,
Renewed our pride in country,
And then came home to a patriot's dream.

Now at century's end, in momentary peace and safety,
We honor you and all your lost friends,
Here on the lovely, lonely plains of southwest Nebraska.
In the center of the country you defended,
A memorial by a traveled road is built for you, our sons and fathers,

A bronze plaque on a concrete star for all your pain:
Blue Star Memorial Highway

A Tribute to the Armed Forces that have defended the United States of America

DEATH OF AN EAGLE
BY
BILL MONKS

I quickly move my pack and cartridge belt as this young kid jumps into my hole. He was a kid. Couldn't have been more than 18 or 140 pounds. I said to myself, this kid thinks the coach sent him off the bench to join the game. He was actually happy to be here. Eighteen-year-olds don't die.

DEATH OF AN EAGLE
By
Bill Monks

Non-Fiction

It was one of those nights you want to lock on to. It was Christmas night; we had just finished a fantastic dinner. My wife and I retired to the family room to enjoy the beauty of the burning logs.

As I sat down with a Manhattan in hand, Dot came over and sat on my lap. I knew after three score ten that it doesn't get any better than this. The grandchildren were deep into their new toys and frolicked on the tufted rug. *Please, dear God, don't let them knock over the tree.* With fifteen grandchildren, twelve of them under eight years, I definitely need a bigger family room.

My seven kids were still sitting at the table talking over their coffee. Two of the girls were lawyers, and from what I could hear, they were expounding on the joy of their clients inheriting fortunes. Jack, my youngest boy, yelled out to me.

"Hey, Dad, did anybody ever die and leave you something?"

"Yes son, about fifty years ago an eagle died, and left me a fortune."

"What did you do with it Dad?"

I smiled. "I still have it."

The kids laughed and went back to their chatter. Who could figure Dad?

My thoughts drifted back to the long ago, the night of my inheritance. It was night, only it wasn't night. The busting of shells and flares kept the sky a bright orange. The light reflected back down off the cloud of smoke that capsuled the island of Iwo Jima. The ground was covered with what seemed like a dense fog: only it wasn't fog.

Thick vapor choked the lungs as the acrid fumes of sulfur seeped out of the pits. Hell was loose. It had escaped earth's bondage. Grotesque bodies lay over the landscape, some partially covered by the black sand. The scene of carnage could only be compared to the last level of Dante's inferno.

I hunkered down for the night, praying, constantly praying. The roar of shells never ending, there was no room for silence. I felt an unbelievable emptiness. They were all dead or wounded: Frenchy, Nose, Kilpatrick, the whole damn squad. I was dead; nothing left but a bag of skin.

"Look out Joe, coming in. Move your gear. I just joined your squad."

I quickly move my pack and cartridge belt as this young kid

jumps into my hole. He was a kid. Couldn't have been more than 18 or 140 pounds. I said to myself, this kid thinks the coach sent him off the bench to join the game. He was actually happy to be here. Eighteen-year-olds don't die.

"Where did you come from?" I asked.

"I'm a replacement off the Funston. We have been out there circling the island for three days...what a show! Now they got the ship packed with wounded. Fifty of us just joined Charlie Company. You must have taken some losses."

"Yea, kid, we took our share. Charlie had 250 when we came ashore. There are only about 40 of us left. Just sit real still kid and welcome to hell. Jeez kid, when did you get out of Boot?"

"About three months ago."

He suggests that we make the hole bigger. I give him two good reasons why we couldn't.

"One you can't dig in this shit and the other is that you will get hit before you got your shovel off your pack."

That night the kid kept talking. He came from a turkey farm outside of Cedar City, Utah. I really wasn't listening, I was thinking of the letter in my pack. The night before, checking the odds of getting off the island, I wrote a letter to my wife and the kids. It was a letter that I prayed my wife would never read. As the kid rambled, the idea struck me to give him the letter. The steel downpour was tearing the hell out of the bodies. There was a good chance that if I went down, the letter would be destroyed. I figured I could use the kid as my mailbox.

It was some sort of insurance. If he went down first I would take the letter back. I got the letter out of my pack and explained to the kid how I would appreciate it if he would carry it for me. The kid was eighteen, and it never occurred to him that he was old enough to die and that he might get hit before me.

As the hours pass, I kind of opened up. I tell him about Dot and the kids: Andy and Megan. I flash the pictures I keep in my helmet. For a moment I'm off the island as I babble about the children.

The kid's all right, but he is so damn young. I can't believe there is a very good chance that he will be dead tomorrow. The kid still doesn't realize where he is.

Son-of-a-bitch, a grenade is in the hole. One of our little brown brothers has lobbed a grenade right in on us. It landed smack between us. I freeze and the kid yells, "I got it." He throws himself on it and snuggles up to that grenade like it's his teddy bear.

He takes the full force of it, tearing him to pieces. I wake up as they carry me aboard the Hospital ship. Shortly after I get home, I receive a letter from his folks. Somehow they got the letter I had written to my wife. I go out to the turkey farm and have a sit down with the family. It was the least I could do, but it was the hardest thing I ever did.

They show me the family album; he seems to be on every page. One picture shows the kid in a Boy Scout uniform. His chest is covered with merit badges. He didn't look any older in the hole. His Dad stares at the picture.

"My boy was an Eagle, the highest rank you can get in Scouting. Come into the living room, we want to show you what the Government gave our boy."

I suspected what they were about to show me. I remembered our Colonel wrote up the report about what happened that night. There it was. The biggest merit badge of all, the Congressional Medal of Honor.

They want me to stay the night but I just can't do it. I keep hearing the kid saying, "I got it."

Did I ever inherit any thing? The kid left me everything.

BETRAYED
BY
STEVEN MANCESTER

The father of two sons and one beautiful, little girl, Steven Manchester is the published author of *The Unexpected Storm: The Gulf War Legacy, Jacob Evans, A Father's Love, Warp II* and *At The Stroke of Midnight,* as well as several books under the pseudonym, Steven Herberts. His work has been showcased in such national literary journals as *Taproot Literary Review, American Poetry Review* and *Fresh! Literary Magazine.* Steven is an accomplished speaker, and currently teaches the popular workshop "Write A Book, Get Published & Promote Your Work". Three of his screenplays have also been produced as films. When not spending time with his children, writing, teaching, or promoting his published books/films, this Massachusetts author speaks publicly to troubled children through the "Straight Ahead" Program. See: **http://www.StevenManchester.com**.

They now say it's all in our heads.
The Lord says they'll reap what they've sown!

BETRAYED
By
Steven Manchester

Inspired by Joyce Riley & Dave vonKleist

A madman invaded Kuwait,
to feed both his greed and his hate.
But no one could stand for the cries-
so WE stood and followed God's fate.

For weeks, we attacked from the skies,
to destroy drums of gas...or the lies?
And swallowed the little green pills,
as businessmen cut their old ties.

Uranium claimed many kills,
while suffering paid freedom's bill.
And though we faced evil—afraid,
each broadcast showed only the frills.

Though justice was all that we prayed,
we never dreamt we'd be <u>betrayed</u>
by those who had sent us to fight;
the same leaders that we obeyed.

Now- truth is a myth, not a right
for Gulf Vets who share the same plight
"So quit all the bitches and moans!"
...get used to the darkness of night.

Remember the big welcome home?
When they swore we'd not feel alone?
They now say it's all in our heads.
The Lord says they'll reap what they've sown!

While thousands are forced to take meds,
the others are dying in beds.
And all 'cause the truth can't be said?
Perhaps what we fought for...IS DEAD.

THE STORY OF ONE SOLDIER
BY
HELEN KAY POLASKI

Helen Kay Polaski has more than twenty years of experience as a professional writer. The mother of three children, she has worked for such causes as the Domestic Violence Project/SAFE House, the Todd Beamer Foundation, literacy, and a Nebraska war monument. She has worn many hats, including author, screenwriter, and newspaper reporter and editor. Currently, she is editor of Adams Media's anthology series, The Rocking Chair Reader.

According to those who knew him, Bill was one of those guys who never let life get the best of him—no matter how bad things got—nor, if he could help it, would he allow those around him to be down.

THE STORY OF ONE SOLDIER
By
Helen Kay Polaski

Non-Fiction

This article first appeared in The Milan News-Leader in 2001 as a Memorial Day Salute to a fallen comrade. Bill Gee was a man about town and respected by those who knew him. The author would like to share this moment with Bill—a man who would have written his own book someday if he'd been allowed more time.

William Kenneth Gee II, a Vietnam veteran and member of the American Legion Gladfelter Post 268 passed away on May 22, 2001 after a long and arduous journey through the horrors of Agent Orange, the ravages of cancer, and the constant debilitation Multiple Sclerosis caused.

Bill is sorely missed. But according to his family, there are no regrets, just a huge sense of loss. His wife, Vickie, loved Bill a lot and misses him terribly, but at the same time she has no regrets.

"We loved each other so much that I know I did everything I could do to make him happy while he was here, and he did the same for me," she explained.

I personally met Bill about a dozen years ago through Vickie, who at the time divided her time between driving a school bus and setting the latest trends in hairstyles at a local salon. Bill, who had already been diagnosed with MS at the time, was the kind of guy you just automatically gravitated toward.

Despite the fact that he leaned heavily on a cane, or if he was having a particularly bad day, was confined to a wheelchair, Bill was upbeat, personable, witty, sympathetic, compassionate, and genuine. Though Bill and I didn't talk or visit on a regular basis, I know that if I had a problem he would always be there for me. He was just that kind of a guy. I swear his heart was the size of Texas.

Over the years our lives brushed against one another many times, and each time, Bill's condition was successively worse. And I couldn't help but notice that his outlook on life, if anything, was brighter. That left a lasting impression in my mind, and as I talked with different individuals around town, I realize mine was not the only life Bill had touched.

He was a big, muscularly built guy, who made living in a wheelchair look easy to the rest of us. As long as he was able, his wheelchair was on the move. On any given Sunday you could spot him as he zipped to and from Immaculate Conception Catholic Church, or high-tailed it up to the park with one of his young grandchildren on his lap. He always had a smile on his face and a devil-may-care attitude.

Bill loved life, and to the extent he was able, lived it to the fullest. And for Bill, that meant family came first. Between the two, they have three boys, Scott Barker, Jason Gee and William Kenneth McGee III, who recently changed his name back to the original spelling—something Bill and Vickie had talked about doing but never got around to. As a Dad, Bill was second to none. He had a good relationship will all three of his sons, and his grandkids were his pride and joy."

Many grandparents make the mistake of spending too little time with their grandchildren. Not Bill. To Bill, time was precious as were his grandchildren. He spent as much time with them as possible. And not just when necessity dictated the need, but also when fun times were waiting to be had by all. Bill was not one to miss an opportunity.

He drove Justin to speech class every morning on his electric cart, and took Ryan to the park. He liked teaching them things, especially about nature. One day he took Ryan to the park, made a fire, opened a can of beans, and they roasted hot-dogs together. With MS, it wasn't easy for Bill to do these kinds of things, but it didn't matter how hard it was, he did it anyway.

When Jason's daughter, Madison Lynn, was born, her mother, Veronica, brought her to Bill every morning at 8 a.m. because he would rather she was with family than in a day care at such a tender age. Bill kept the baby happy until Vickie got back from her morning bus run at 8:45, then she'd take over. When Madison was about four months old and more rambunctious, Bill, who was steadily losing strength in his hands, decided it was time she started attending day care.

"He just wanted to spend as much time with her as possible—he loved that little girl," said Vickie. "When she got older, she used to sit on his lap in the bed and they'd watch cartoons together. She always tried to help me take care of him."

Not only was he close to his grandkids, but also to his sons.

When Bill became gravely ill, Scott, who was living in Alabama, moved home so he could be here to help me and to be close to his father, as well as the rest of the family. Then Jason and Billie took off work and remained by their father's side.

"None of us regret it one bit," said Vickie. "We decided we didn't care where the money came from. Bill had always been there for us, and we wanted to be here for him. The boys later said to me that they know their dad through and through, and not everyone can say that about their father."

According to those who knew him, Bill was one of those guys who never let life get the best of him—no matter how bad things got—nor, if he could help it, would he allow those around him to be down.

Longtime family friend, Alan Hale, admits he's never met anyone with a better outlook on life.

"He had the most incredible sense of humor," said Alan. "And any one of the neighborhood kids could have called him Dad. He'd take them under his wing if they needed help."

Pat Kiger, another friend, agrees. "He was a very inspiring person for my own children," she said. "He was like a brother to me and whenever my kids needed a friend, uncle, or another adult they could talk to, Bill was always there for them."

Tricia, Pat's eldest child, relied heavily on Bill when stress got the best of her, and depicted Bill as her second father and hero in various college essays. Daryl, Pat's second child, also respected Bill and thought of him as a father figure.

"Bill was a big football fan, so whenever the Milan High School football team won, Daryl would have the bus stop in front of Bill and Vickie's house and the kids all hung out the window and screamed the Big Red chant," said Pat. "Bill loved it and the kids loved it. Last year they invited Bill to the banquet as an honorary guest and gave him a white football with all of their autographs on it, and the Gee's gave them each a key chain. Daryl asked to borrow the football for his senior pictures in remembrance of Bill and what they shared throughout high school."

Though Bill was eager to help everyone else, he didn't ask for many favors for himself. When it came to his health, he did not ask for preferential treatment, nor did he receive any.

Bill was also an aspiring writer and shared my goal of one day having a book published. We promised one another that if and when we reached that goal, whoever finished first, would drop off an autographed copy at the other's home. Though Bill wasn't able to accomplish his dream, he was on the right track. He was always writing something.

"He'd write stuff and then have me read it back to him to see how it sounded," Vickie said. "I teased him about writing a book, but I always read his stuff. Some of it was pretty good. His mother had written a book called *The History of Petersburg*, and he wanted to do something similar. He and his mom were very close, writing was one of the things they shared."

In 1976, Bill's father, William passed away. Shortly afterward, his mother, Virginia, was diagnosed with MS. Since doctors told the Gee family the disease wasn't hereditary, they hadn't expected Bill would end up in the same boat, but after a while Bill started exhibiting the same telltale symptoms.

"I remember when we were dating, he always complained that his hands were constantly going numb on the steering wheel," Vickie recalls. "But the doctors said people with head injuries were most susceptible to MS, and Bill had gotten a severe head injury in the Vietnam War. So, no, we weren't really surprised when he was diagnosed."

It was hard for the family to watch Bill suffer through the same agony his mother had been through and Vickie says she would have done anything to make things better for the guy "with attitude in his step."

"When I first met Bill, I didn't like him," she admits with a chuckle. "He always walked with such a high and mighty attitude! He acted as though he could conquer the world and I thought, 'oh, forget you.' I wouldn't have believed that anyone who walked with such a cocky attitude would be someone I would be attracted to. But as it turned out, his walk was just his outlook on life. He really did have the confidence to back up that walk, but it wasn't the 'I'm a bad guy' attitude you'd expect would accompany that kind of strut."

Later, when walking was only possible with a cane, Vickie realized how important the little things in life really are. She would have given anything to see Bill's confident strut again, but that's not the way MS works.

She turned toward the window with a far away look in her eyes. "MS is a disease and all it does it take, take, take."

The price Bill paid for serving his country from 1967-68 as a United States Marine in the Vietnam War was a head injury, which probably was the cause for his MS. But even without a head injury, Bill's health would have declined once he returned stateside.

"While he was fighting for our country, our government dumped tons of Agent Orange, a chemical used to kill the foliage, on the area," Vickie explained. "It was a jungle-like terrain, so the Agent Orange cleared the wooded areas and did help our service men at the time, but if we'd known what it would do to them later on, we'd never have used it."

Fifteen years later, Bill suffered through angioplasty, and the loss of one kidney, which began forming cancerous lesions. His doctor's confirmed the illness was one of the complications of Agent Orange exposure.

"I don't know what it did exactly, but Bill said after a spraying, the bananas grew to humongous proportions and the animals dropped dead like flies. He said as soon as he saw that he knew it wasn't good for humans, but what choice did he have?

"There was no way to avoid it, and he didn't have time to think about it, really, he was in combat for his life. He said he knew one or the other was gonna get him."

After a long, hard-fought battle and miles of red tape, Bill and Vickie were finally awarded government compensation for their suffering and eventually received a one-time amount of $500 for the suffering the Agent Orange caused. Though it was not much compensation, the Gees felt lucky that was the only problem Bill had suffered.

But regardless of the complications and illnesses, Bill stayed optimistic. He never had harsh words to say to his family or to anyone else. His unconditional love extended beyond his family and he accepted everyone for who they were, and when his disease kept him from helping others, he turned his puppy dog eyes on his wife. And she couldn't resist his few requests. She tried to fill in the gap and help everyone Bill wanted to help.

In retrospect, Vickie isn't sorry about one single thing regarding her life with Bill, except how the government handled their responsibility in regards to his illness.

"When Bill asked me to marry him, my mother asked me to take a long hard look at the situation," says Vickie. "Everyone knew he'd had a head injury and that head injuries can come back to haunt you later on in life. But because of the love he gave me, I was willing to take that chance. I said I'd take what I could get out of life and be happy, and at least for a short period of time we had all of that happiness."

Vickie and Bill would have been married for 30 years in December 2001. He was sick for twenty of those years.

Vickie smiles and nods her head. "When I think back, I realize God works in mysterious ways. Maybe it was good that we had hard times—it kept us close."

AN AIRMAN DIED TODAY
BY
MARGARET MARR

Margaret Marr lives in the mountains of western North Carolina where she spends her days working for Shannon Taylor Trucking and her nights for Southwestern Community College.

She's a multi-published author of paranormal novels with romantic elements. Her next release, *Wings of Thunder*, will be available from Publish America in late 2005 or early 2006. Margaret is also a regular contributor to the e-zines *Seven Seas Magazine* & *Nights and Weekends*.

When she's not working her two jobs or writing, she spends time with her two boys. She likes to hike, swim, camp, and fish in the dark. While her boyfriend is away serving in the Air Force, Margaret shares her bed with two mommy cats and five kittens that like to hog the pillow and blanket when a cold wind is blowing outside.

Visit Margaret Online at:

http://margaretmarr.bravehost.com/index.html, or drop her an e-mail at: **mizz_scarlett@hotmail.com**.

Are you there God?
How is my soldier?

AN AIRMAN DIED TODAY
By
Margaret Marr

Late afternoon rain falls,
a lullaby for my troubled mind,
a quiet peace for my trembling heart.
Lost in sleep I try to forget
evil turmoil in soulless places

An Airman died today...

Are you there God?
How is my soldier?
Is he still nestled in your loving hands?
He's still tucked in my heart, and I
offer a million prayers for his safe return.

YOU'RE IN THE ARMY, BUD
BY
ORVILLE "BUD" WOHLER

Orville Wohler, better known to his family and friends as Bud, was born in Riley County Kansas where he has lived all his life except for time spent in the army. His parents were farmers, and had a family of 10 children with 3 dying in infancy. His ancestors were all of German descent. He farmed for 25 years, until health problems forced him to take other employment. He was married in 1944 to his neighbor girl; they recently celebrated their 61st anniversary. He has two daughters, two sons-in-law, two grandchildren and 4 great grandchildren, all the joy of his life. At 88 years of age, my theory is: "Be patient with me –God isn't finished with me yet."

Orville Wohler, US Army

On 7 December 1941 we were told that the Japanese had attacked Pearl Harbor and had landed on Kiska and Attu Islands. We were to report to supply and draw a rifle. When I got there, they shoved a rifle at me. We had a ten-minute class on the Browning Automatic when we were at Camp Callan, and now I didn't have the slightest idea how to fire the thing.

YOU'RE IN THE ARMY, BUD
By
Orville "Bud" Wohler

Non-Fiction

In 1940 my dad traded off the Model A for a '34 V8 Ford so I could haul my sisters around. It was also the car I drove when Phyllis and I had a date. We didn't do too much, just a movie in Waterville now and again. But, I loved that car and when I was leaving for the Army, I sold it to Barney and Babe for $90.00 and a red heifer calf. Dad kept the calf for me while I was in the service. She was grown and had calved twice by the time I got back home.

There were a lot of weddings the winter and spring of 1940 – 1941 since the draft had started. Phyllis and I were going together pretty steady then, but we didn't think much of getting married to dodge the draft. After all, I would only be gone a year and we could wait. I am glad I didn't know it would be four years and four months before I got back.

There wasn't a big crowd to see me off when I left home on June 22, 1941. I boarded the bus in Washington, Kansas, on the way to Omaha. We picked up guys in several towns along the way. My cousin was in the first group to board the bus in Washington and he was the only one I knew. After he took his physical the next day, he was classified 4F and sent home, but I was on my way.

At camp, we were standing around waiting – something I got good at – when some guy in Army clothes came up and told me to go with him. Not knowing any better, I went. He led me to a supply room and gave me a broom, mop, bucket and rags and told me to get busy cleaning the latrines. I didn't even know what a latrine was but soon found out. It turned out that this guy was a private assigned to latrine duty and he just passed the job on to me. That never happened to me again.

Soon, we were given physicals and shots and were sworn in on 25 June 1941 and bused to Ft. Leavenworth, Kansas. The next day, we were on a train headed for California. Since I had worked with horses and livestock most of my life, I was sure that I was headed for the Cavalry. I was relieved when I ended up at the Coast Artillery Camp at Camp Callan near San Diego, as a gunner.

We were quarantined for the first two weeks and couldn't leave camp, but this didn't bother me. I didn't have any place to go, anyway. Camp Callan was built right next to the Pacific and the guns were on a cliff overlooking the ocean. We were allowed to climb down to the beach on our time off and we could swim in the surf. It was a pretty stiff climb back up so I didn't go too often.

We drilled everyday on the parade ground, in sand halfway up our ankles. We had "dry runs" firing the big guns and finally fired them for real when basic training was over. That was the only time in the 52 months I spent in the Army that I got close to the 155's as they were firing.

In October 1941 we all fell out in ranks on the parade ground and were told we were being sent either to Alaska or to the Philippines. Supposedly, we had a choice and most of my Battery voted to go to Alaska. I doubt that our vote had anything to do with it but, in less than a week, we boarded a train for Seattle, Washington. We traveled through orange groves and vineyards and, whenever the train stopped, the workers picked oranges and grapes and piled them on the train for us. That was good eating. I enjoyed the trip since I had a lower bunk all by myself. This was one time it paid off to have a name beginning with "W". Everything goes in alphabetical order in the Army, so I was the last one on the train.

It never rained while I was in California but when we got to Seattle it was cold and wet. It drizzled every day while we waited in old stone barracks with no heat. After several days, we boarded a freighter, a relic of WWI, and spent most of a day sitting in the harbor. We started out just before dark on a beautiful calm evening. I stood on the deck until late and thought this trip was going to be great. I went to bed only to awaken sometime in the night to realize that things were no longer calm. We had sailed out of Puget Sound and were on rough open sea. When it was time to get up the next morning, I stood up and the world turned upside down. I dashed for the railing and had a tough time finding an empty spot. I learned that a person is better off up-wind from seasick people.

The ship had not been built to haul troops but someone had rigged it with bunks stacked two high. The next night out we hit a storm and the old freighter bounced around like a cork. Our quarters doubled as the galley and there were about 30 big stainless steel containers filled with potatoes and other vegetables sitting on the floor. As the ship rolled from side to side, these containers started to slide and finally one of them crashed into the side of one of the lower bunks. The man sleeping on the bunk was doused with 25 gallons of water and potatoes. It sure broke the monotony of the trip.

After about a week at sea we arrived in Seward, Alaska, which was a mistake as we were supposed to be in Kodiak. There was a camp in Seward so they put us up in tents for a few days. Our barracks bags were sent on to Kodiak so we had no other clothes but what was on our backs. There was snow on the ground and each tent had a little wood-burning stove in it burning pine, which was a real nice smell.

Soon another ship came to take us on to Kodiak. We docked outside the town and got into trucks to travel to our new home, a tent city. Civilian contractors had hauled smooth round rocks in and compacted them with a bulldozer. The rock layer was about two feet deep, laid over volcanic ash eight to ten inches deep. The contractors hadn't put any sewer pipes of any kind down before the rocks, so it was clear that they could hardly wait for us to get there. Our first job on Kodiak was digging sewer trenches by hand, through rocks and volcanic ash.

We were assigned four guys to a tent with wooden floors and shiplap boards on the sides and a regular wooden door. There was a wood burning stove and two sets of stacked bunks. It rained most of the time and the inside of the tent was sopping wet by morning. The guy in the top bunk moved very carefully to avoid touching the canvas or he got as wet as the canvas. There were a few barracks built for the infantry and if we wanted to walk the ¾-mile over and back, we could shower and shave in relative comfort. It was a long walk in sub-zero weather so I took mighty few showers that winter.

On 7 December 1941 we were told that the Japanese had attacked Pearl Harbor and had landed on Kiska and Attu Islands. We were to report to supply and draw a rifle. When I got there, they shoved a rifle at me. We had a ten-minute class on the Browning Automatic when we were at Camp Callan, and now I didn't have the slightest idea how to fire the thing. Since my job was in the wire section of communications, I was hopeful that I wouldn't need to use a rifle and, for the most part, it stayed in the truck as we strung wire all around Kodiak Island. The next weapon we were given was the new Girand rifle. We were told to carry it with us, no matter what. We were stringing wire through tall grass and bushes, in all kinds of weather. You can imagine what those new rifles looked like in a short time. It was impossible to pass rifle inspection with them so we were then given a little Tommy gun to carry. If it was raining, it stayed in the truck.

Stringing wire in winter was a challenge. If the wire ran through forest, there wasn't too much snow. If it was out where the sun could hit the deeper snow, making a crust of ice on top, each step broke through into knee-deep snow. One day, after going through the icy crust all morning, I started getting leg cramps and finally I couldn't lift my foot out of the snow to move on. My buddy was doing better than me and was able to stomp out a path so I could make it to the timber. It was pitch black by the time we made it back to the truck and the next time we had to go out to check wire in the snow, we had snowshoes.

We had building inspection every Saturday. On Friday nights we scrubbed the board floors until they were bleached almost white by the time we left Kodiak. After the floor was dry, we put papers down and the last thing we did as we left on Saturday morning was take them up. Late one Friday night we could hear a mouse on the papers. We all lay there in the dark trying to decide how to catch it. We thought we knew what corner the mouse had come in and since I was closest to the light switch,

I turned on the lights and another guy, who usually slept in his birthday suit, covered the hole in the corner aiming to smack the mouse with his shoe. The mouse headed for the corner and the man covering the hole tried to hit it with his shoe, missed and finally chased the mouse around the floor, bent double and whacking at it with all his might. The mouse met his demise, we plugged the hole and it was the only mouse we ever had. I will never forget the comedy and laughter of that night. It is set to music in my mind when I think of it.

After thirty months, the rumor we had been hearing about going home was finally coming true. On 16 March 1944 we got word that we were to be on the ship to go home. We got into the trucks, drove onto the pier and boarded. The trucks may still be sitting there for all I know. I never looked back.

Once in the States, I made my way back to Kansas City by train, took a bus to Topeka, got a taxi to where Phyllis was and we had a great reunion before heading home. I gave her the ring I had brought from Kodiak and we decided to get married the next Saturday, April 22, 1944 if it was agreeable with everyone. Guess it was or else everyone has been holding his or her peace for a long time.

I didn't get to stay home. Ten months later, I was on a British ship sailing out past the Statue of Liberty on my way to Germany, docking at Liverpool, England, on 18 February 1945. While waiting for orders, we were able to go on tours of the city. We saw Winchester Cathedral, a thing of great beauty with stained glass windows hundreds of years old, the colors as bright as new except for one piece that had been replaced with more modern glass. It had faded and showed that the ancient glass could not be replicated. Walking around London, we saw that many places were boarded up because of the bombing. Winchester Abbey was boarded up and sand bagged. We watched the changing of the guard at Buckingham Palace and I knew that was a job I would never have enjoyed.

In time, we headed for France, crossing the English Channel and traveling up the Seine River. There were signs of battles that had been waged. Tanks, armored cars and trucks, all burned and now rusting away, were evidence of a horrific struggle. We beached the boat and were put up in a big tent camp. We were issued new equipment and driven to Brussels, Belgium. Since I had a "blue card", I was one of the drivers of the half-ton trucks while others drove 1½-ton trucks. We made quite a convoy on the way back into Germany.

We crossed the Rhine River into Germany on 30 March 1945 at Aachen, which had been completely wiped off the map as it was on the German Zigfield fortified line facing France and their Magino Line. There were a large number of German troops in the area, cut off from any supply lines by the advance of the Allies. The area was known as the Ruhr Valley and it was so cold sleeping in the open field, I was covered with frost in the mornings. We were finally able to find housing and, except for when standing guard, able to stay warm and dry.

We had been bored with our guard duty until one night the shelling began. They were coming in every three or four minutes, some off to the East but some very close. It only lasted 45 minutes but seemed an eternity. During that shelling, I made the Lord some promises that I'm pretty sure I haven't totally kept.

I don't remember where we were when the Germans called it quits in May of 1945. All I know is that I was a long way from home. We traveled to Frankenforst, Germany, in order to set up our Battalion Headquarters. The citizens of the town were moved out, taking only their clothing and bedding and whatever they could carry. The houses weren't damaged by artillery or bombing so it was really nice compared to army barracks or tents. Our wire section had a couple of houses and I had my own room with a bathroom.

The country close around Frankenforst was mostly untouched by the war, but just a few miles up the river was the city of Cologne, almost blown off the map. A big church with twin steeples could be seen for miles and this was about the only building in Cologne that was still standing.

After a time the British Army took over the area so we could move out. We left around 15 June 1945, driving the Auto-Bohn. It was the first time I had ever seen a highway and we made good time. The only problems were the detours since every overpass and bridge was blown out. We stayed just outside Stuttgart in the town of Heilbron, which had been the site of a horrendous battle. From the stench of death, it was the final resting place for many.

In the end, I was short two points for discharge but, thanks to a vote to receive a star for exceptional service, I ended up with five more points, more than enough for me to begin the process of going home. While waiting, some of us went to Paris, just to say we had been. It sounds like a big deal to say I was in Paris! Shortly after the Paris excursion, we heard on the radio that the atomic bomb had been dropped on Japan and the war was over.

Almost everyone had an enemy rifle they had picked up and were supposed to turn in or get rid of. There was an outhouse in back of some of the houses and that is where a lot of those rifles were laid to rest.

We left France 26 September 1945 and stayed in England a very short time before we were on our way to New York and home. It was another rough crossing and many men were sick the entire way. We finally came into New York Harbor, traveled up the Hudson and then dropped anchor. The Red Cross ladies were waiting with milk and donuts, the first fresh milk in months. We turned in our equipment and had our last physical. At the separation center, all those going to Ft. Leavenworth were called and we were on our way. The morning after arriving there, we had our last pay call and then received our discharge papers, a long wait since I was still at the end of the line.

Phyllis met me in Topeka and we went home...there truly is no place like home.

HOPE
BY
MIKE WHITNEY

Mike's Top Five Big Deal Moments:

1954 I wrote and performed in a sci-fi play broadcast on the radio. Dad taped it. Age ten.

1956 Heartbreak Hotel hit number one. I was dancing with Renee Durand in her basement when somebody put it on.

1964 Ed hosted the Beatles that Sunday night. Picked up the guitar.

1969 I wrote two songs and, in 1970, the second one got lots of airplay in Cincinnati. Road bands and solo gigs followed for the next 33 years.

2004 home is the sailor, home from the sea, and the lizard, home from the lounge.

3 CDs on CD BABY – **http://cdbaby.com/all/mikewhitney**
Web Front Door - **http://www.dnet.net/user/mlwhitney/**

Hope you live forever

HOPE
By
Mike Whitney

Hope you live forever
Hope you always have a home
Hope you live with the one you love
Hope you never live alone

Hope your smile comes easy
When tears begin to fall
Hope what you do that comes back to you
Is your best time of all

Turn to me when you need a friend
I will turn to you and in the end

Hope your load grows lighter
and you grow stronger every day
Hope you live with the ones you love
Hope the children learn to pray

Turn to me when you need a friend
Remember times like these and in the end
Hope you live forever

WATERLOO
BY
F.G. MCCANN

Born August 1946—like a lot of children as a result of the war ending. Work for Sefton M. B. C. (Local government) Joined the Air Cadets in 1959. Stayed there until I was twenty-three. Qualified as a glider pilot but only after crashing one. Became, and still am an expert shot with the old British Army .303 service rifle. Won a number of cups for shooting. Joined Liverpool Police Reserves (Special Constabulary) in 1967, and served for just under 20 years, reaching the rank at one time of Inspector. Served through two riots. Retired from them and went to work for Sefton, which is a metropolitan council north of Liverpool. For the last 15 years, I have been Attendant to His Worshipful The Mayor of Sefton. My job is his driver macebearer bodyguard, and among other things Executioner. (Not practiced) My hobbies are reading, writing, and falling off my mountain bike, but only at speed while coming down the side of moorland hills. Married to Margaret, who is my strong right hand, since 1969. Have two children Karen (Terri) 33, and Stephen 31, and three grandchildren.

The sentries kept turning everybody out. They were shooting at shadows. Men in uniforms could be seen approaching in the darkness. Challenges were made and unanswered shots were fired, and, nothing. No return fire—nothing. The shadows would vanish, only to appear a few moments later.

WATERLOO
By
F. G. McCann

Non-Fiction

During the Second World War, my father served in the finest fighting force in the world. How do I know this? He told me so. From 1939, until he was invalided out in 1945, my father was a British Royal Marine. Now if you ask any marine, anywhere in the world they will tell you that the marines are the finest fighting force anywhere. My father was in the British Royal Marines therefore he was in the worlds best.

When The Second World War started, he decided although married with a child on the way, to enlist before conscription caught him up. That way he could choose whom he joined. His size and strength would otherwise see him drafted into the infantry. As he approached the army recruiting office, Dad had to pass the Royal Navy recruiting office. He stopped to look at the posters and found himself talking to a large Royal Marine.

"Join the army," The man said. "A man with your build and bearing? Are you mad?" He pointed to his dress uniform. "Now this is the force for you. The Royal Marines."

So, my father found himself a member of the world's finest fighting force. (His words not mine) He was sent down south for his training, but in 1940, while still undergoing training, he and his comrades found themselves being taken out of camp and sent to the south coast of England then placed aboard small ships and boats to cross the English Channel. The British and French Armies were being taken off the beaches of a French Port called Dunkirk. His job along with the other marines was to assist in the evacuation. Any marine will tell you that the two prime duties of the Marine Corps are (1) Stop sailors from getting into trouble, and (2) Get the army out of trouble. My father and his comrades were about to take part in number 2. They landed on the beaches and the harbor and for a number of days stayed there loading wounded and controlling the troops as they waited to be taken off. Remaining calm although every bone in your body screamed at you to turn around and run for the safety of the evacuation ships.

The army saved, the marines returned to barracks and their training. For the rest of the war, the company would stay together apart from the usual transfers, promotions, and deaths. In war death is much a part of life.

After the thoughts of invasion by the Germans faded my father found himself with his company posted to North Africa where they would fight their way up and down that small stretch of coastal strip of land between Cairo and Tripoli. In 1942, along with thousands of others, he started the long advance from a small railway station in the middle of nowhere. Until that day, nobody outside of the 8th Army had ever heard of a place called El Alamein. Now it ranks with places like Waterloo, Gettysburg and Stalingrad, as places were the tide turned forever.

Dad and his stayed with the 8th all the way through to Tunis. Then in 1943 they landed along with many others in Sicily. Still, in most part, the same company that had left England. Later, they would land in Salerno then later at Anzio.

Orders came that they would be going home. The Second front was about to happen, so that meant another beach and beaches meant marines. His company spent their last night, before embarking for home, in an orange grove. When they left the next morning, most of the oranges had gone. The people of England had been rationed for years. My father arrived home with an extra kit bag full of oranges. After getting off the train at Liverpool Lime Street Station, he boarded a tram to take him home. A young lady taking the fares asked him for his. My father explained that he had just arrived home, and had no change for the fare. The Clippy (Female Tram Conductor) insisted that he paid or left the tram. My father reached into his kit bag and pulled out a fresh orange. Something that had not been seen in England since The War started.

"Will this do?" He asked. He told me that the young girl's eyes almost popped out of her head. He could imagine her taking it home that night and showing this thing of wonder to her family. Then her mother would look at her and ask. "What did you have to do to get that?"

In June 1944, my father and his company once more found themselves heading for a beach. This time it was Normandy. The Second Front had opened. They fought in the hedge rows and fields then when the break out came, they fought their way up through France chasing a German army who every so often would turn back and snap at the forces following them.

Each night it would be the same routine. Find somewhere to sleep. A barn, a farmhouse, a village or set up your tents in an open field. Cook a meal, set the sentries, and try and sleep. Always half awake in case of counter attack. Then just before dawn stand too and watch the shadows. If no attack came, cook breakfast.

So it was this night. The company set up camp in an open field somewhere on the French Belgium border. A meal was cooked, and sentries set. Then the rest of the company settled down for the night. The first thing my father noticed about that night was you could not sleep. The sentries kept turning everybody out. They were shooting at shadows. Men in uniforms could be seen approaching in the darkness. Challenges were made and unanswered shots were fired, and, nothing. No return fire—nothing. The shadows would vanish, only to appear a few moments later. Thus set the scene for the whole night. A number of times my father had just dozed off when he awoke startled convinced he was not alone. He would swing his rifle towards a uniform figure just seen out of the corner of his eye only to have it vanish before he could aim.

As dawn approached, the company stood too and waited. Waited for that attack that they knew was coming, for had not the German Army spent the whole night probing and wearing them down. Sure enough, in the mist, uniformed figures could be seen. But as you aimed your rifle at them they seemed to vanish. Then a cry would go up "Over this side." But they too would vanish.

Dawn came, the mists vanished and the expected counter attack never came. A very weary company set to cooking breakfast. As they did, the sentries reported a civilian approaching—a local farmer wanting to trade fresh eggs for tea or coffee and maybe some sugar.

"Good morning Gentlemen," he said. "Welcome to my country. Thank you for throwing the Boch out. Did you sleep well?"

My father, being a good Scouse (Liverpool) Person and so not known for being shy, replied, "No, we did not. Where the hell are we?"

The elderly farmer looked at my father, then at the other marines and smiled. "But gentlemen, this is Waterloo. You are camped on the old battlefield." With that, and his trade complete, the old man walked back towards his farm.

Was this a case of long dead soldiers coming to visit their live comrades on a battlefield that had seen much suffering? Or was it a case of other troops moving up through these seasoned troops? Moving so quietly that they made no noise? Troops so well trained that when fired on did not return fire. What do you think?

My father was invalided out of the Royal Marines in 1945. He went through six years of war without a scratch, and then with almost the last shots being fired he broke one of the main rules of any marine. Ask any marine anywhere in the world, and he will tell you. The two most dangerous things in the world are sailors with guns. If God had meant for sailors to have guns he would not have invented the marines, and the most dangerous of all, officers who think they know what they are doing.

The company received a new officer—a straight-out-of-training-I-know-what-I-am-doing officer. He insisted that this day he was going to drive the Jeep. He did. The result was he put it into a ditch upside down and almost killed the four of them in it. That was the end of my father's war. He suffered from those injuries almost to the day he died. But, once a marine, always a marine. He went to meet his maker wearing his blazer with his Royal Marine badge on it. I know he went to Heaven, because as we know, God is the ships captain, and all captains need marines to keep the others in order.

What was that line?

Another marine reporting sir. I've served my time in hell.

AT LEAST HALF
BY
ARTHUR C. FORD, SR.

Arthur C. Ford, Sr. was born and raised in New Orleans, La. He earned a Bachelor of Science degree from Southern University in New Orleans, where he studied creative writing and was also a member of the Drama Society. He has visited 45 states in the United States and resided for two years in Brussels, Belgium (Europe).

His poetry and lyrics have been published in newsletters, journals and magazines throughout America and Canada. His next book, Reasons for Rhyming (Volume 1), will be released in the near future.

Mr. Ford currently resides in Pittsburgh, Pa. where he continues to write, edit and publish poetry and prose. Contact him at P.O. BOX 4725, PITTSBURGH PA. 15206-0725, E-mail: **arthurford@hotmail.com**.

My daughters, my daughters, my sons, my sons

AT LEAST HALF
By
Arthur C. Ford, Sr.

At least half of WWII Vets' daughters and sons,
fought the Vietcong,
Proving history repeats itself,
Wrong begets more wrong.

At least half of the Vietnam Vets' daughters and sons,
were sent to the Middle East,
Proving mankind eats mankind,
our children are our feasts

Persistency in dying
through generations of daughters and sons,
While mothers at home are crying
and spouses carry burdens in tons.

Fathers' daughters wait for their sisters
and brothers
Kids weep for their dear old moms and dads,
Boyfriends write letters to lassies,
girlfriends pensively want their lads.

The blood just takes on surnames,
traditions just don't care.
Count the daughters and sons of WWI Vets
In WWII at least half of them were there.

My daughters, my daughters, my sons, my sons
Embrace your daughters and sons,
For they are going, even though many have been
And we know not what their plight may be
Or what war they will fight in.

My daughters, my daughters, my sons, my sons,
I know not what war means,
I only feel it'll never cease
Until Jesus intervenes.

WHY I ATTENDED THE USS COLE MEMORIAL
BY
SHANNON RIGGS

Shannon Riggs is a US Navy officer's wife. She works as a writer and college writing instructor. Visit her website at **http://shannonriggs.com**. This essay first appeared in *Proceedings* magazine.

When we arrived, the skies were dark grey, threatening rain. I zipped my son's bright yellow rain coat and thought the color was too bright, too cheerful for a day like today. Maybe we shouldn't have come.

WHY I ATTENDED THE USS COLE MEMORIAL
By
Shannon Riggs

Non-Fiction

I didn't know any of the sailors who were lost or injured in the recent attack on USS Cole. Still, this past Wednesday, I found myself grappling with the decision over whether to attend the memorial service or not.

My husband serves onboard the Dwight D. Eisenhower, not USS Cole. I heard on the morning news that the injured Cole sailors would all attend the service, as well as some of the families of those who perished.

I almost decided not to go. I didn't want to appear as if I were ogling the injured sailors and grieving families, like a rubber-necker driving past a traffic accident; I have too much respect for what these sailors and their families have given up. Also, my four-year-old son, not yet in school, would have had to come to the service with me. I worried that he wouldn't understand and that he'd act inappropriately.

Somewhere deeper down, I also worried that he would understand.

As I made my way down Hampton Boulevard toward the Navy base, two thoughts kept crossing my mind, like the refrains of a hymn. The first was that this could have happened to my family and me. My husband just returned August 18th from a six-month deployment. The second was that it <u>wasn't</u> me, and did I even belong at this memorial service?

Still, I drove on.

When we arrived, the skies were dark grey, threatening rain. I zipped my son's bright yellow rain coat and thought the color was too bright, too cheerful for a day like today. Maybe we shouldn't have come.

As we edged our way through a sea of crisp, white uniforms and somber faces, a reporter from the New York Times called out to me from the sidelines. He wanted to know if I knew any of the Cole sailors.

"No," I said.

Then he wanted to know why I was there and why I had brought my young son with me. I looked up at my husband's ship towering over us. Just a couple of months ago, it wasn't there.

"My husband serves onboard the Eisenhower," I said. "They just got back from deployment a couple of months ago."

But why did I feel the need to be there, in person, at the ceremony, the reporter wanted to know. In asking, he merely voiced what I'd been asking myself all morning.

"Because when my husband was out to sea, every time I baked cookies for a care package, every time I sent a love letter, what I was really saying was, 'Please God, don't let this happen,'" I said. "And then two months ago, I stood on this pier and took part in a Homecoming party. What I was really saying then was, 'Thank God this didn't happen.'" I looked back at the reporter, scribbling his notes. "And now, dear God, it <u>has</u> happened, and I just couldn't stay home."

Then I told him what we all say. The Navy is a big family and we pull together in times of crisis.

Wednesday night, my husband came home from work.

My husband came home from work.

We cooked dinner, washed dishes, put our kids to bed, and went to bed ourselves. I kept thinking of the spouses of those who died who were going to bed alone that night—that night, and every night from now on. I thought of those who would never have the chance to marry and raise a family of their own.

In the darkness of our bedroom, I recalled the words of Secretary Cohen from earlier that day. "No one should ever pass an American in uniform without saying, 'Thank you. We're grateful.'"

Suddenly, I realized why I felt so compelled to be at the memorial service in person. And although part of it was the very public reason of wanting to express my sorrow for the losses of the USS Cole sailors and my respect for what the injured have given, I found my true reason was much more private and personal.

"Do you know why I went today?" I asked my husband.

"Why?" he said.

"I went for you. I want you to know that I don't take what you do lightly." Finally, after an entire day of questioning myself, the answers spilled forth. "I didn't want you to think that I don't respect and appreciate the risks you've taken. I wanted to go in order to honor <u>you</u>."

My husband was quiet for a moment, but then he whispered, "Thank you" in the darkness.

Secretary Cohen was right. Every service member should have this kind of moment. I hope each of the lost sailors of the USS Cole, at least once, had this kind of moment.

BLACK TUESDAY
BY
ELIZABETH CLEMENTS

Thousands died that Black Tuesday
In buildings and planes and rubble,
And in just eighteen frightening minutes
Unholy men burst Freedom's bubble.

BLACK TUESDAY
By
Elizabeth Clements

The sky blooms like a vivid rose
Of perfect cerulean blue,
Not a cloud mars its pristine state;
Two tall buildings pierce the view.

The towers stand for commerce and trade,
A tribute to engineering skill,
Yet on September 11th they became targets
Of a madman's plot to kill.

The first plane caught New Yorkers by surprise
When it ploughed through glass and steel
But minutes later a second plane proved
This nightmare was deadly real.

This isn't a horror movie spewing
Clouds of choking dust
But a tragedy of gigantic proportions
All because of one man's lust.

Our hearts grieve for the men and women
Who braved the flames and fears
Saving countless lives, but lost their own,
For them we shed our tears.

And we weep, too, for the volunteers,
The firemen and policemen who toil
Through ash and death and crumpled steel
That litter America's soil.

No human being should have to face
What these people see each day
Lifting not just shovels of lumpy ash
But bits of lives now crushed and grey.

Thousands died that Black Tuesday
In buildings and planes and rubble,
And in just eighteen frightening minutes
Unholy men burst Freedom's bubble.

For how can terrorists call themselves holy
When in God's name they kill and maim?
And because of evil they wrought that day
Our world will never be the same.

Yet the human spirit is strong and will prevail,
Those thousands will not have died in vain;
Around the world nations are merging
Against evil, injustice and pain.

Yes, the skies are blue again above the skyline
Of New York's shining towers
And the sun shines brightly, but all else is changed,
Gone is the innocence that was ours.

THE WAAC CARAVAN
BY
DEBORAH M. NIGRO

Deborah M. Nigro, (D.M. Nigro, Deborah Mona) welcomes the challenge to create quality material for readers of all ages. A Cape Cod resident born and educated in Boston, she is a feature writer, teacher, bookseller, and the author of popular novels published in the U.S. and Europe. Network news anchor Paul Zahn interviewed Deborah for a television feature on the romance industry. Her work has appeared nationally in *First for Women*, *Highlights for Children*, the Macfadden publications and many other outlets. *John F. Kennedy: The Promise of Camelot* (amazon.com), a condensed biography for family reading, was approved for sale by the National Park Service. Deborah's e-novel for young adults, *The Wolfman, the Shrink and the Eighth-Grade Election* (Twilight Times Books) reached the Fictionwise.com Top 20 Young Adult bestseller list. Fictionwise is the world's largest retailer of electronic books. Contact Deborah at: P.O. Box 2072, Hyannis, MA 02601.

Women are vitally needed to fill clerical, technical, medical and other roles so that more men can be freed for combat missions. Here in New England, we're organizing a special series of fifteen recruiting shows we're calling the 'WAAC Caravan.'

THE WAAC CARAVAN
(pronounced: wak caravan)

By George Anthony Nigro
As told to
Deborah M. Nigro

Non-Fiction

In the spring of 1943, I was just another anxious army private stationed at old Fort Heath, in Winthrop, Massachusetts, on the shores of Boston Harbor. Like the rest of the GIs in the Coast Artillery, I woke at dawn to the sound of 'reveille' being blasted on a bugle. Usually off-key. Then I marched, endured deafening cannon training, pulled cleanup patrol, stood guard duty, and marched some more, all the while dreading the arrival of those orders that would send us overseas. To where? To what? It wasn't an easy time.

But there was one great thing about Fort Heath: I got to blow trumpet in the volunteer band. We enjoyed playing for the lively Saturday night dances. Sometimes, it was even me blowing 'reveille' to jolt the guys out of their bunks.

We must have sounded pretty good, because one morning, the battery commander approached us in the mess hall to make an announcement. "Major Walter Brown and some more brass from the First Service Command are coming to give you guys an audition. He needs a hot band for a special assignment. They'll be here at fourteen-hundred hours..."

"But sir, that doesn't give us much time to set up and rehearse," I blurted out.

"That's right, private. So what are you waiting for? DisMISSED!"

A special assignment? We hustled to the recreation room to tune up our instruments. Big Band music was all the rage. Glenn Miller, the Dorsey brothers and the King of Swing himself, Benny Goodman, were our idols.

Right away, we swung into our best number, the sophisticated and thrilling, 'Brazil.' I loved playing solo on that one. I had a way of sliding my fingers over the trumpet keys that sounded just like Tommy Dorsey. Our Saturday dance audiences were crazy about it. We hoped Major Brown would be, too.

Standing at attention in our sharpest olive-drab uniforms, we were as ready as we'd ever be when our visitors arrived. Major Brown wasted no time in explaining the assignment. It went something like this:

"Recruiting at least 375,000 young women for the Women's Army Auxiliary Corps, better known as the 'WAACs', is a top priority of General Eisenhower's. Women are vitally needed to fill clerical, technical, medical and other roles so that more men can be freed for combat missions. Here in New England, we're organizing a special series of fifteen recruiting shows we're calling the 'WAAC Caravan.' The chosen band will tour with us to cities and college campuses from Maine to Connecticut, helping the WAAC recruiters to sign up female volunteers. There'll be radio stations, parades and celebrities involved. Big stuff. Now, let's see what you can do."

We didn't sound as smooth as we had during rehearsal. Nerves, I suppose. It didn't help that the major barely smiled through the first two songs. By the time we finished 'Brazil', he was actually frowning. Not a good sign.

But we didn't have to wait long for his decision. Major Brown nodded briefly toward our battery commander, and then grinned broadly. "Excellent, gentlemen," he said. "We've found our ideal band. You'll have your itinerary shortly. I know you'll make this important tour something to remember."

We were in! On April 5, in a flurry of publicity and high hopes, the WAAC Caravan hit the road.

Over thirty military trucks emblazoned with the WAAC logo rolled into the industrial city of Lynn, Massachusetts, for the kickoff show. And what a show it was!

At noon, escorted by the magnificent Fort Devens color guard, military police and officers, three WAAC units in smart khaki uniforms marched through the heart of the city. Maxie Armstrong's 366th Infantry Orchestra, a popular African-American group, played rousing patriotic tunes. Screen star Ralph Bellamy hosted a national radio broadcast right from English High School auditorium, site of the main event. By 7:30 show time, all 1,500 seats were filled. Hundreds more people, too late for tickets, actually stormed the lobby.

With the WAAC recruiters positioned at tables on every side, the curtain rose to the inspiring strains of the National Anthem. Several WAACS displayed their vocal talents with songs like 'Indian Love Call' and 'Saint Louis Blues.' Military comedy skits brought gales of audience laughter. The famed Fort Devens Symphony Orchestra added a touch of class. Poetic readings and a WAAC uniform 'style exhibit' showcased 'the best-dressed women in America.'

After that, it was our turn. We did 'Alexander's Ragtime Band,' and of course, 'Brazil.' I'm proud to say we got almost as much applause as Maxie Armstrong's outfit! The whole company ended the program with a booming chorus of 'Marching Along'. Judging by the cheers and the number of young women flocking to the recruiting tables, the caravan was going to be a huge success.

It was the same way at every stop: music, crowds and enthusiastic recruits. In Quincy, Massachusetts, a detachment of precision marchers from the Royal Australian Air Force, resplendent in bright blue uniforms, joined our parade. We were treated like today's rock stars, but we never let it go to our heads. Our purpose was to support the WAAC's vital recruiting efforts, and we took our role seriously. The 'farewell spectacular' was held at the 16,000-seat Boston Garden arena. We damned-near filled the place! The WAAC Caravan has been called, 'the biggest all-service show ever produced.' When it was over, the letdown was equally big.

Back at old Fort Heath, I gazed out onto the grey waters of Boston Harbor, once again pondering my uncertain future. Those freezing nights in flimsy tents on the Rhine River; the strafing bullets that barely missed us on a picturesque German street; blowing trumpet at an allied service dance, where I met the lovely British army staff driver who became my wife - none of those things had happened yet. Looking back, I wouldn't have missed them for the world. But then, I was still that worried GI, uneasy about what was to come.

And those eager young women our music had helped bring to the W.A.A.C.? Soon they, too, would be stationed far and wide, away from their families and the security they'd always known, facing the enemy in the Big War.

STREET SCENE
BY
DENNIS J. SMITH

Dennis J. Smith is a semi-retired schoolteacher who lives in Cedar Falls, Iowa. He teaches instrumental music part time at a small parochial school in that city. Writing is an avocation; he is by training and profession, a composer of music, doing numerous pieces for several web sites the invitation of dear friends. He has a daughter, 20 years old and two step sons who are now "out of the nest" and have families of their own. His hobby, not often visited these days, is drawing realistic graphics in various media.

in the war torn street, one leg folded beneath him,
he cries.

STREET SCENE
By Dennis J. Smith

she does not cry,
the child maybe three, maybe four years old

his shoulders betray a sense of surrender,
the way he cradles her small form in his arms

      toes on bare feet slightly curled, blood
      has seeped through soft, pink clothing
      her delicate complexion olive-brown
      coal black hair drawn back, from her face
      dying eyes, half open, seem to study the place
      where her tiny hand lies on his camouflaged chest

a red cross on white field marks his helmet,
someone else's M16 lies next to where he sits

in the war torn street, one leg folded beneath him,
      he cries.

PRAISE FOR THE WOMEN WHO WAIT AT HOME
BY
MARY EMMA ALLEN

Mary Emma Allen writes for many inspirational publications and anthologies. Currently she's working on a children's novel based on her ancestor's experiences during the Civil War era. She grew up during WWII and relates these memories for her daughter and grandchildren so they'll have an appreciation for the men and women who have kept and currently are keeping our country free. Visit Mary Emma at **http://homepage.fcgnetworks.net/jetent/mea**.   Email: **me.allen@juno.com**.

Uncle Al served in the Army Air Corps during World War II. This bachelor son, who wasn't needed on the farm, traveled further from home than any family member to help secure his country's freedom.

PRAISE FOR THE WOMEN WHO WAIT AT HOME
By
Mary Emma Allen

Non-Fiction

War has affected women since time eternal, when sons and husbands left their families to defend homes and country. I've discovered many women in my family were touched by the wars to keep our country free throughout the generations.

As I read letters written by great, great grandmothers, I realized how much the Civil War altered their lives even though they lived far from the fighting. The concerns and heartbreak come through words written nearly 150 years ago by great, great grandmother Cynthia Irish Banks.

"I will put in Henry Ira's letter as I have no time to write about him. I want thee to keep it till I come [for a visit from Illinois to New York State] as I keep all his letters as a precious jewel," Grandmother Cynthia wrote to another son, my great grandfather Willis, and his family in 1862.

In another letter she wondered how long Henry and a younger son, Egbert, would be fighting in "Mr. Lincoln's war."

My grandmother, this lady's granddaughter, waited for her son during World War I. As I looked through memorabilia of Grandma's life, I found a small flag...two red stripes on either side, with a white one in the center and blue star on the white. I recognized it as Uncle Charles' flag.

Many years before I was born, my father's brother served in World War I, in a cavalry unit after he graduated from veterinary college in 1918. I recalled my mom telling me about the flag that Grandma, my father's mother, hung in the window in recognition of a son at war.

Grandma had packed the small flag in a trunk with Uncle Charles' military uniform...remembrances of that earlier war when a son served while she waited for his safe return.

World War II saw another grandmother waiting for a son. A heart shaped pin with "Mother" scrolled across in gold remained among her memorabilia. Hanging from the script was a tiny golden heart with a tiny stone in the center.

When, as a child, I asked Nanny about her pretty pin, she told me it reminded her to keep Alfred in her prayers. Uncle Al served in the Army Air Corps during World War II. This bachelor son, who wasn't needed on the farm, traveled further from home than any family member to help secure his country's freedom.

I remember Nanny waiting for news of Alfred stationed in the Pacific during World War II. She and my mother treasured letters from him, letting them know he was alive. Those years were long and worrisome for Nanny with Alfred away as an aircraft mechanic. He came home uninjured while many soldiers didn't for their mothers.

A maternal great, great grandmother did lose a son in the Civil War. Uncle George died near Atlanta, after following his regiment throughout the Washington, D.C, Virginia, and Gettysburg areas, then west to Tennessee and back east to Atlanta for three years. He never made it home, dying of dysentery after the Union Army marched across the South.

Her letter to her daughter was full of heartbreak. I had it with me when I visited Uncle George's grave at the Union Cemetery in Marietta. I hoped I was completing a journey my great, great grandmother Eliza couldn't make to pay homage to her son and find closure.

As a former military wife, whose husband was an Air Force pilot during the 1960s, my heart goes out to these ladies of years ago and mothers, wives, and fiancées today waiting at home, that "invisible" military force supporting the troops who keep our country free in battlefields around the world.

INFINITE LOVE
BY
ELIZABETH CLEMENTS

Long, suspense-filled days;
the agony of waiting....
SILENCE.

INFINITE LOVE
By
Elizabeth Clements

The singing of the blood
through lovers' heated veins,
surging...passion's flood...
sublimely, sweet love reigns!
BLISS!

Then blazing battle guns
sweep terror through the land...
enlisting brave young sons-
so scared, he strokes her hand.
PARTING...

Long, suspense-filled days;
the agony of waiting....
SILENCE. Then in a daze
she reads the letter, stating,
...HEROIC DEATH!

SHATTERED! Pain-filled days
in her barren room,
as to her God for death she prays
then...*JOY!* For in her womb-
LIFE!

THERE AND BACK
A Tribute to John Paul Plese
BY
LORI ZECCA

Lori Zecca is the author of numerous works, including the award-winning contemporary novel *Love Enough for All*. She is co-contributor to four anthologies, and a freelance writer featured regularly in several monthly trade magazines, of which, incidentally, requires travel that inspires her muse. Self-described as a Mad Hatter, Lori is an active member of the Romance Writers of America and her local chapter, MORWA, a lecturer and essayist, and often her own publicist. When she isn't writing or reading, she loves to paint, garden, and otherwise create. And, until she can fulfill her dream of seaside residence, she lives happily with her husband and son in St. Louis. Visit her on the Web at **http://www.lorizecca.com**. Email: **lorizecca@yahoo.com**.

Sergeant John Paul Plese
United States Marines

He was a young and idealistic man of the times, willing to honor God, family, and country, with little regard to himself.

THERE AND BACK
A Tribute to John Paul Plese
By
Lori Zecca

John Paul Plese, known to most as "Jack," is an American war veteran. This is his story.

Intrigued by the many stories I had heard over the years from his adoring, and extremely proud family, who portrayed Jack as a spunky senior with unique charm and the occasional strength of mind, I relished the prospect of meeting him, if for no other reason than because of my friendship with his daughter, Bonnie Knapp. However, after spending a delightful evening with Jack and his lovely wife Jean, listening to his many tales of days gone by, it became abundantly clear—friendship aside—Jack Plese was a man worthy of my interest on any level.

Jack Plese was born in *Helper*, Utah on October 22, 1921. Ironically apropos, considering his eventual tour of duty with the United States Marine Corps, as he served to protect the freedoms of American citizens in World War II. He was a young and idealistic man of the times, willing to honor God, family, and country, with little regard to himself.

With the 1939 conflict between Germany and France escalating to include most of the world's nations by 1941, Jack joined the United States Marines as Private First Class with the 6th Defense Battalion. Proud as he were, it was an ominous point in time, as the U.S. had just abandoned its neutrality in the European war, and was now approaching confrontation with Japan in Asia and the South Pacific.

Stationed first at Midway Island in the South Pacific, Jack was transferred to Pearl Harbor for a short tour of duty before being reassigned to the 10th Defense Battalion and finding a home at Henderson Field, just north of Guadalcanal for the next thirteen months. The war in the south Pacific had really heated up following the assault on Pearl Harbor, and even though the Battle of Midway had stopped the Japanese from further infiltration in the central Pacific, they advanced instead to the southwest Pacific.

The travesty at Pearl Harbor struck an exceptionally raw nerve for Jack, having been stationed there briefly. The onslaught was that much more personal, wounding in a way that was as bothersome to him forty years later, as it had been to him then.

It had been more than a year since the attack on Pearl Harbor and still the Japanese occupied Guadalcanal at the southern end of the Solomon's chain, a series of islands in the south Pacific, and a vital Japanese air base. By midsummer 1942, the United States directed the naval and ground forces in the southwest Pacific to drive the Japanese out of the Solomon's and northeastern New Guinea, and the 10th Defense Battalion was called into action. On August 7, 1942, the U.S. infiltrated

98

Guadalcanal, and as the Marines battled the Japanese in the unbearable tropical climate, the Navy simultaneously fought in the waters surrounding the island for the next seven months. Despite the lengthy expanse of time and many casualties, whether due to combat or malaria, the U.S. secured the Guadalcanal in early 1943. Following this victory, Jack was sent to the Marshall Islands, located in the North Pacific Ocean, where he and his battalion played a crucial role in the attack and securing of Enewetak (also known as Eniwetok or Eniwetak).

As the end of 1944 approached, Jack was sent stateside first to San Diego before being ordered to the 1st Separate Radio Intelligence Platoon in early 1945 for training on Bambridge Island, located in the state of Washington. Taking his instruction with him, Jack was then transferred to Maui where he prepared for the invasion of Japan. It was there, the now Sergeant, Jack Plese joined the Headquarters of the 5th Amphibious Corps.

On April 1, 1945 the U.S. 10th Army, composed of four army and four marine divisions landed on Okinawa. Even though the Japanese had created strong defenses on the southern tip of the island, the U.S. secured the northern three-fifths of the island in less than two weeks, and the rest by the end of June. By August 1945, President Harry S. Truman issued orders for atomic bombs to be dropped on Hiroshima and Nagasaki consecutively. Jack was amongst the first troops (the initial occupation force) to enter the Japanese naval base at Sasebo following the U.S. attack. However, in December 1945, Jack found himself stateside once more at the Oak Knoll Naval hospital in San Francisco, where he suffered from a mild heart disorder and sheer exhaustion.

Jack's final assignment as a Sergeant in the United States Marines encompassed a much-deserved rest and recovery period at the Washington State Naval hospital, until he was discharged in June of 1946. It was during this time that Jack met, courted, and married his adoring wife, Jean, after which they raised two daughters, became grandparents of several treasured grandchildren, and maintained wedded bliss for nearly fifty-nine years.

Always a vital member of society, Jack retired from an impressive career with Anheuser-Busch, reaping the many rewards of his golden years in Arizona, playing golf every chance he was able, and still managing to give his grandson, Jonathan some stiff competition.

The precision in which Jack communicated his part in American history is not only a legacy to his family and future generations, but to the memories of those who fought beside him that weren't as fortunate as he, and those who have since passed on. They are heroes in every sense of the word, representative of what our country stands for and the irreverence we refuse to accept. In light of the unfathomable events of September 11, 2001, we have been all too cruelly reminded of how vulnerable we have become and how precious freedom is. Our veterans of all wars have fought to secure the freedoms we have unwittingly taken for granted, and now more than ever, their efforts should not conclude in vain but unite us as Americans, as we hold tight to the liberties our veteran's have so valiantly served to protect.

Sadly, Jack did not live long enough to see the result of my many questions. He knew about this tribute and was very pleased, though succumbed to illness on December 24, 2004 before it had come to print. His daughter, Pam Tarvin, who provided invaluable information to this historic account, once said that her father had never been honored for his duty during the war. I beg to differ. Jack honored himself by keeping the memories alive, and now as his story reaches all of you, he is honored again as each of you take his memories to heart.

God, bless our nation, keep us strong and resourceful, skillful and forgiving, and above all, bless the souls of our armed forces who have, and continue to protect all we as American's hold dear.

MY DAD, MY HERO
BY
ANN MARIE BRADLEY

Ann Marie Bradley inherited her love of books and writing from her mother, and her interest in creative writing stretches back to when she was a child. Her favorite type fiction combines her love of cats and the paranormal. These days her stories are far from traditional romances. Each heroine has a pet cat, based on one of the author's own cats.

Ann spins tales of love and intrigue, with heroes to die for. Reality shifts behind dangerous shadows, delves into the past through time travel or reincarnation, and always sweeps you away through the realm of sweet romance and imagination. Ann has won many awards and contests for her writing, and has been published in magazines and newspapers. She is currently working on a novel-length manuscript, FOREVER OVER ALL. She also has a non-fiction short story published in the anthology, LET US NOT FORGET, a tribute to America's 20th century veterans, and has written radio commercials. You can read excerpts of Ann's work on her web site at **http://www.annmariebradley.com**.

Private First Class John F. Ross

Dad never bragged about his part in the war, or even mentioned it to me.

MY DAD, MY HERO
By
Ann Marie Bradley

Deep in my heart, I feel very strongly that everything I've accomplished in life has not been by my own efforts, but as a gift from loving parents. Like most little girls, I worshiped my father. Long before he was a hero in my eyes, he was a true hero of World War II. I wasn't even born when he boarded a boat with hundreds of other young GIs, to cross the Atlantic on their way overseas. He left behind a pregnant wife and their young son. She kept newspaper clippings and letters, and that's where I get my information.

Training and fortitude kept my dad active in the 65th Infantry Division. The last weeks of the war against Germany were fought as much with 21/2-ton trucks as with weapons. In thirty-nine days, the division traveled 500 miles. It was a continuous battle of transportation. Two days before V-E Day, Dad won the Bronze Star Medal for bravery. The Citation describes his deed in part:

"On May 5, 1945, near Leonding, Austria, a convoy of Company 'K' (260th Infantry Regiment) was subjected to an intense 88mm artillery barrage. The men dismounted from trucks and sought cover. Realizing his truck was in the center of the artillery concentration and knowing the value of the vehicle to the company, Private First Class John F. Ross left his covered position and ran to the truck.

Disregarding shell bursts, he climbed into the cab and drove the truck to a position of cover. His courageous action saved the vehicle from probable destruction and materially enabled the unit to continue on its mission with the least possible delay.

His cool bravery and quick thinking reflect great credit upon himself and the military service."

Dad never bragged about his part in the war, or even mentioned it to me. He died at the early age of forty-nine from heart failure. I was eighteen.

I've grown into an adult with children and grandchildren of my own. I have his army photo, medals, and flag in prominent display in my home.

A fierce surge of pride grows in my heart and I thank all military personnel for my freedom and way of life. Because of men and women like my dad who fight to keep this country free and strong, I live with peace of mind, love without fear, and enjoy the good things in life. Love, hope, faith, and a bright future wait for my grandchildren. I watch America's flag fly over the world's greatest nation, and thank God it's still there.

AN AMERICAN FLYER
BY
BARBARA BALDWIN

Barbara Baldwin was born in California, married in Iowa and now resides in Kansas. The years in-between were lived in most of the southern states and 3 in Japan because her father was an Air Force pilot. That probably explains why she still loves to travel and explore new places and has each of her manuscripts set in a different locale. She has written practically all her life, beginning with journals of family vacations. She is now published in poetry, short stories, essays, magazine articles, teacher resource materials, and full-length fiction. Of course, her writing is sandwiched in-between playing a little golf, traveling and a full time job. Barb loves talking almost as much as she loves writing, and has been a teacher for grades K-8. While in education she made over 100 presentations at state and national conferences on material she had developed in the classroom. Later, during 14 years with public television, she was on air as a program moderator and during annual pledge drives. She has a BS in Education and an MA in Communication and has taught public speaking classes at the college level. Barb can be reached at **writer0926@yahoo.com** or through her Website at **http://www.authorsden.com/barbarajbaldwin**.

Lt. Carol D. Norris, USAF (about 1946)

"The flag in your window." I nodded my head in that direction as I spoke. "Care to tell me about it?"

AN AMERICAN FLYER
By
Barbara Baldwin

This is a story based on actual events during the Berlin Airlift in which my dad flew.

I was looking for a story. Temporarily stuck in a small, Midwest town as I followed the presidential campaign hopefuls, I needed something to do between a pancake breakfast and the Kiwanis's lunch. This was my second loop around the town square, peering into shop windows, wondering if I should buy the postcards portraying pigs in sunglasses. The girls back in the office would really think I had lost it then.

Although an avid political reporter, I could use a personal interest story. I turned down a block of neatly trimmed lawns and carefully kept homes. I sighed. I kicked a stone down the sidewalk. Just when I began to think a nap would be more productive, I found what I was looking for.

In one corner of a bay window was a newspaper cutout of the American flag. Beneath it were the words "Proud to be an American". In an age of flag burning and questioning of the American government, this symbol really stood out. Even in a nice suburban town straight out of the sixties.

I jaywalked toward a man sitting in a lawn chair. His feet were kicked out in front, his fingers laced together across his generous middle. The Pioneer Seed cap he wore blocked my view of his face.

"Excuse me?" I tilted my head to the side and took another cautious step forward.

"I see you." He tipped the cap back and I gazed into the clearest, bluest eyes I'd ever seen. Black hair, graying at the temples, and skin so baked by the sun it looked like dried leather made it hard to determine his age.

"The flag in your window." I nodded my head in that direction as I spoke. "Care to tell me about it?"

He squinted, as he looked me up and down. "You must be one of those reporters; here to cover all the election stuff."

"As a matter of fact, I am, but that's not why I stopped."

"Good, because I wouldn't vote for that no good so and so. After all, he went to a foreign country and protested our being in Vietnam and what do we do – elect him president. What damn right does he have to run our country when he did that?"

"Why the flag, then? Were you in the military?"

He shifted a little straighter in his chair. "Lt. Col. Carol D. Norris, USAF, Retired."

"OK, if you don't want to talk politics, tell me about your years in the Air Force."

He didn't appear at all comfortable talking about himself.

"Do you have any newspaper clippings of that time?" I often ask for newspapers because through the shadows of time, a person's memory of particular happenings gets out of proportion.

"You'll have to ask Mitzi. She was the letter writer all those years. Knock on the door; she'll tell you."

Mitzi smiled and invited me inside, happy to tell me about her husband of fifty years. She showed me a desk against one wall of the dining room. Buried in the back corner of one drawer were numerous yellowed clippings. Historical documents, originally sent home by a proud wife, reprinted in the local paper by an equally proud mother.

Perhaps here I could find the source of his courage-- the reasons behind his stalwart belief in America. I read and discarded, until I found that particular article that showed the beginning, but perhaps not the end, of what makes an American.

Lt. Carol D. Norris, son of Mrs. Lillian Norris, has received a citation for the Air Medal. As pilot of transport-type aircraft, he successfully completed over 100 missions from bases in Germany to land-blockaded Berlin in connection with Airlift, Operation 'Vittles.'

The citation reads: "Confronted with a difficult schedule, restricted to flying precise time, often under adverse weather conditions, this officer's efforts resulted in the delivery of many hundreds of tons of food and supplies essential to the lives of 2,500,000 people. His determination and skill in the performance of hazardous duty reflect the highest credit upon him and the United States Air Force."

"Why did he do it?" I whispered in awe.

"It was his job -- his duty -- as a member of the United States Air Force," Mitzi stated without hesitation. "But more, it was his dream to fly."

Fate had led me to the right house. I punched the button on my tape recorder as Mitzi told his story --the dream of an American Flyer.

* * *

May, 1946 - Frankfort, Germany

Lt. Carol Norris was shipped to Germany and Mitzi followed in October. During the next year, they moved three times. He had been trained as a pilot, but in Erlangen he was a housing officer. Not a difficult position, but he longed to be high in the sky, touching the clouds.

He had dreamed of flying after hearing stories about barnstormers in the twenties who swooped and rolled through the sky. There had even been a plane land at Pimple's farm just north of the main road one summer, offering to take people for rides just like the barnstormers used to. But he was working and couldn't get away right then. By the time he arrived, breathing hard because he had run all the way, the biplane had already taken off for the last time.

A thin trail of white vapor was the only evidence the plane had been there at all. Carol angrily shoved his hands into his pockets, releasing the two quarters he had clutched in one grubby fist. He had hoped to buy a ride. He didn't even know if he had enough money, but he had selfishly saved for months in the hopes that a barnstormer would come to town at County Fair time.

Carol shook off wayward thoughts of his childhood as he approached the T-6 trainer that a maintenance airman was preparing. The airman saluted smartly and Carol returned the acknowledgment. The move to Zepplinheim and then Roth had been fortuitous. He was now flying trainers; testing them before he trained other young pilots. Younger even than his twenty-two years.

Summer, 1947 -- Landsburg, Germany

Carol Norris was satisfied with his life, yet restless. In the back of his mind, there was an elusive need to do something. After all, he was only twenty-three -- in his prime -- and he longed for an adventure.

Then, in June of 1948, everything changed. In a last ditch effort to control the divided Germany; Russia blocked all entrances to Berlin, thinking the Allied Forces would buckle under to demands. Ground forces and over 200,000 civilians in the western sector of the city were left without supplies. Food would run out in a day.

The Russians, however, made the mistake of allowing three airways, each only twenty miles wide, to remain free of interference. The Allied Forces in the French, British and United States sectors of Germany had only one recourse. They mobilized what Americans called "Operation Vittles". Flying twenty-four hours a day, in all weather, flight crews and airplanes maintained a steady flow of food, coal, and equipment into the cordoned off sector of West Berlin. And Lt. Carol Norris was right in the middle of the excitement.

September, 1948 -- Wiesbaden, West Germany

Sweat trickled down his back beneath his flight suit. The tiny fan pivoting just above his head in the C-47 provided little relief from rising temperatures. Heat waves wiggled up from the concrete between the nose of his plane and the tail of the one in front of him; and the one in front of that, and so on down the line.

Carol couldn't even see the beginning of the line of C-47's. They remained stacked on the taxiway, single file, waiting their turn to take off. His stomach churned as he recalled the briefing held at 0600 hours that morning.

Radio reports were calling the combined airlift task force under Maj. General William H. Tunner one of the greatest feats in aviation

106

history. What the Russians didn't think could be done, the United States Air Force, with the help of the British, were attempting to accomplish.

Every three minutes a plane took off, allowing Carol and his two-man crew to inch the loaded plane forward until they had to stop and wait again.

"Damn the waiting," Carol swore.

"It's better than in the beginning of the Lift," his co-pilot, Andy, replied. "Hell, they used to stack us up four hours at a time. Now it's only an hour."

"Yeah, well, I want to get up and get back. The weather's suppose to change. I'd rather have visual than rely on radio and radar to land at Tempelhof."

Silence fell over the three in the cockpit, each recalling the crash of another plane just the day before. Considering the extreme conditions in which they sometimes flew, they were lucky not to have more accidents than they did. No matter, the loss of even one crew meant a lot to the other young pilots who were part of the Berlin Airlift.

Carol had wanted an adventure, but now he wondered if this was more than he had bargained for. Precise schedules had been constructed; his flight time monitored down to the very second as he flew over signals at Darmstadt and Aschaffenburg. Only 1,000 feet of air space cushioned his plane from the one below and another above him as several tiers of loaded cargo planes flew into West Berlin only minutes apart.

Man, it was no wonder he was sweating! He could do it, he kept telling himself. This was what they had been trained for. But on days like this, when he became impatient with the waiting; when the weather became unpredictable; he questioned why he did what he did.

He glanced to the top edge of the windshield where he kept a picture of Mitzi, tucked away but always visible. He thought of his wife and baby daughter and knew he would do anything to protect them. Could he do any less for the women and children caught in the web of politics and international intrigue still being played out by the Russians? Not just Allied ground forces had been caught inside West Berlin. Thousands of civilians remained trapped when Russia suddenly closed all entry to the city.

"Red-3-6-7, you're cleared for take off," the control tower squawked over the headset. The adrenaline immediately pumped through his veins and he knew it was more than duty to country that kept him flying. Nothing could top this rush of excitement each time the flight number echoed over the headset; every time his hand steadily pushed the throttle forward and the plane barreled down the runway. No instruction manual had ever captured the feel of incredible force that lifted him into the air to soar among the clouds.

"Red-3-6-7, passing Fulda Range Station at precisely 0900 hours;

speed one-seven-zero, altitude six thousand feet," his co-pilot radioed the information back to the next plane in line.

The patterns set for flying the corridor from Wiesbaden to Tempelhof required controlled speed. Only fifteen minutes separated his aircraft from the one directly in front, or the one just behind. Any deviation from the established route could lead to disaster.

If he couldn't land on the first approach, he'd have to return with a full cargo. There wasn't time for a second try. There wasn't time for a mistake.

In addition, some days the twenty mile wide corridor didn't seem near enough space to maneuver around barrage balloons allowed to drift into the air space, or to evade "buzzing" by Russian fighters.

Carol kept the plane on schedule, and in precisely forty minutes, he received altitude settings and time check for Tempelhof. Within minutes, he landed and taxied off the runway onto the apron. Luck belonged to Lt. Norris's crew that day and even the flight back to base was uneventful.

The Airlift continued nonstop through 1948 and into 1949. Lt. Norris was transferred to Fassberg, but still fought against Russian suppression by tirelessly flying supplies.

Today, the windshield wiper click-clacked a steady rhythm, ticking off the minutes as they once again waited on the taxiway, this time in pouring rain. Always waiting, Carol moaned, thinking of Mitzi as he had left her that morning. Because of the weather, he had refused to let her come to the base with him. She had cried, afraid that breaking their routine would somehow bring him bad luck.

Carol had laughed at her superstitions, but now he reached down to touch the pocket where he kept his wallet. Tucked securely between two pictures was the two-dollar bill he and some buddies had written on each check ride they took during training. He carried it with him everywhere -- not because he was superstitious, but for good luck. There was a difference. Mitzi had nothing to worry about. A little rain wouldn't stop them.

"Red-3-6-7, you're cleared for takeoff."

As he flew, he forced himself to concentrate on every little task. He kept close watch for familiar rooftops or chimneys as they passed over in the torrential rain. The fixed location transmitter blinked in the misty distance; Carol checked his watch and confirmed their position. When they landed at Tempelhof and his co-pilot and navigator got off the plane, he lightly tapped Mitzi's nose in the picture.

"See, I told you nothing would happen. We're good, and nobody can stop us." But his words didn't stop the gnawing in the pit of his stomach that something was not quite in synch.

Only forty-nine minutes after they landed, their cargo had been unloaded. Now, they taxied out and became airborne once more, heading home through the central corridor. The weather hadn't cleared at all, and by the time they passed the last signal and flew into the free western sector, visibility had dropped to zero.

They were put in a holding pattern over Fassberg, circling as ground crew took care of some complication.

"Tower, this Red-3-6-7, request priority handling to the field. Low on fuel."

"Red-3-6-7, continue to hold."

The three men in the cockpit monitored the ground traffic, listening intently for some indication the tower hadn't forgotten of their existence.

Time passed.

"Tower, this is Red-3-6-7. I don't know what kind of emergency you have on the ground, but unless we can have an alternate approach, you'll have another emergency on your hands." Carol was frustrated at the delays. Even more bothersome was the needle of the gas gauge dropping by the minute.

"Roger, Red-3-6-7. Alternate airport at Celle can take you. The weather's even better there. Heading two-two-five degrees."

Carol breathed a sigh of relief as he climbed to a higher altitude. Within minutes they were on final approach at Celle, coming in over the field as directed by the tower.

"Left engine out!" Blake shouted from behind.

Carol swiveled his gaze out the window, then down at the dozens of dials in front of him. "Left throttle idle! Left mixture cutoff! Left prop feather!" He shouted instructions to his crew.

"Damn!" The expletive barely left his mouth when the plane tilted crazily to the left. Without the thrust created by the engine, the plane became precariously off balance and hard to control. Thank God they were empty. The additional tons of cargo would have created an even greater inequity, for it would have shifted with the lurch of the plane.

"Control tower, this is Red-3-6-7 on final approach," Andy radioed in. "Left engine out, all other gears in tact and working."

"Roger, Red-3-6-7, emergency vehicle will be standing by."

Carol's knuckles were white as he gripped the controls and applied steady pressure to bring the plane in under control. He could barely hear the screech of tires on concrete above the pounding of his heart.

For long, hold-your-breath minutes the plane tilted heavily on the left wheel, then the right wheel came down, and finally the tail settled to the runway. It sure wasn't a textbook landing, but Carol could at last breathe as he pulled the throttle back.

"Well, boys, another uneventful run across the border and back," he joked with his co-pilot and navigator as he prepared to taxi to the hangar and catch a ride home. He heard a sputter, then dead silence.

"We just lost number two," Andy said.

"We only have two," Carol replied, mouth turned down at the thought of what could have happened if they had been airborne when the second engine quit. C-47's weren't built as gliders.

"Yeah, well, then there were none." Blake recited, his voice more like a reverent prayer.

Andy radioed Base Ops for a tug that came and slowly ferried them off the roll out and back to the hanger. Carol knew it wasn't mechanical failure that had stopped the engines. They had been out of fuel—bone-dry—empty.

And though Lt. Carol Norris didn't consider himself superstitious, he also realized perhaps his luck had run out. He'd flown a hundred missions down the corridor and back with no major mishaps. It was time to go home.

On the night he was to fly out, he found himself standing beside the runway, watching as plane after plane took off, wing lights blinking steadily until they were swallowed by the inky night. On each take off, his heart soared skyward with the roar of the plane.

One last time, he stood at the edge of a green meadow, wishing he could have hurried a little faster to get there before the old biplane had left. Now, he looked down at his fist, clutched so tight his blunt nails bit into his palm. Slowly he opened his hand, the dim light winking off the quarter his fingers revealed.

Laughing, he flipped the coin high into the night sky. As it became lost in the misty haze of runway and taxi lights, he knew he had finally realized that dream.

The dream of an American Flyer.

SAM'S LEGACY
BY
GRIFFIN T. GARNETT

Griffin T. Garnett was born August 15, 1914 in Washington, D.C. Garnett received his BA from the University of Richmond in June 1936. He then moved to Washington, D.C., attended evening classes at the National University Law School, now a part of George Washington University Law School, and attained his LLB in 1940.

Garnett married Harriet Waddy Brooke of Washington, D.C. in September of 1938. They have two grown sons, one in the law practice with Griffin, and another who is a civilian industrial engineer with the U.S. Navy. Griffin also has three grandsons.

In 1940, Griffin opened his law practice in Arlington. His legal career was interrupted during WWII by his two-and-a-half year stint in the U.S. Navy. While in service, he saw active duty in the S.W. Pacific, serving first as executive officer and later as commanding officer of two landing ships. He left active duty, as a Senior Lieutenant, in 1946, and resumed his law practice.

Griffin's interest in Journalism and creative writing stretches back over many years. He was, during his college days, a freelance writer for the Richmond News Leader. At college, he co-wrote, directed and produced two original musical revues. While at law school, he was, for a period of years, a five-day-per-week statistical columnist for the Washington Times Herald. During his legal career, he originated, co-wrote, directed and produced the Arlington County Bar Association's annual satire. More recently, several of Griffin's creative writings, *Tales from Orchard Point*, have been published in *Pleasant Living*, a Virginia regional magazine. *The Sandscrapers* is the first published novel by the author, followed by *Taboo Avenged*. Visit Griffin at: **http://www.thesandscrapers.com**.

Though he was accepted as one of the boys, he wasn't, and most of the crew, including the officers, sensed Cooky B was someone different.

SAM'S LEGACY
By
Griffin T. Garnett

Fiction

PROLOGUE

12 June 1949

When you have read **Sam's Legacy** *you will know why the narrator of the novel invited me to write this prologue. And, why I was delighted to comply.*

Marcus A. Bosconovich reported for duty on board the U.S.S. Landing Ship Medium (L.S.M.) 460.5, in late June 1944. The vessel, a two hundred three foot oceangoing amphibious assault ship, was tied up for major repairs at one of the docks of the Norfolk Shipbuilding Company, in Norfolk, Virginia. I was then an ensign and her executive officer, later her commanding officer.

One cloudless morning during those dockside repairs, while I was working with Yeoman Troy Bell, the ship's clerk, arranging studies for seamen who were striking (studying) for an advance in grade, Marcus was escorted to the yeoman's office area by Eric Henekin, Chief Gunner's Mate. I merely glanced at our new crewmember, but I could tell he was a well-built blond, cocky, self-assured with mischievous, sparkling, hazel eyes.

"Good morning, Sir," he said, and dropped his personnel folder on the yeoman's desk and left. Troy Bell looked at the folder, and then showed it to me. Marcus A. Bosconovich, then twenty-six years old, had been trained at the Bainbridge, Maryland Naval Training Center Cooking School. His personnel jacket, under "previous occupation," read "Professional Gambler—House Dealer."

"Do you believe that?" asked Bell.

I replied, "Who knows, it takes all kinds to make a crew."

Several days later, while shipyard workers were tearing the guts out of the engine room, I roamed our sea-going mistress checking on various matters. I noticed many of the crew were sullen as all hell. Just before 1100 hours, I returned to the wardroom and was sitting alone at the table preparing reports, when there was a knock on the wardroom door.

"Enter," I said.

Marcus Bosconovich slid gracefully down the ladder handrail. He came over to me, his eyes sparkling good humor. "Sir, after I came aboard and gave the yeoman my personnel jacket, word got to the crew that the new smartass cook had faked his occupation on his personnel record. I didn't mind the kidding, but when they began inferring I was a liar, I decided to call their bluff. I know, as does every other member of the crew, that gambling and cards for money are against Navy regulations. But, what the hell are a bunch of guys going to do on this bucket with time on their hands and no women? So I kinda' inveigled five of the supposedly best card players, backed by crew money, into a little poker game. They now believe what my file says. I made a record of every dollar I took from each player. Here's the take, four thousand three hundred and sixty-nine dollars," he said, handing me a galley cookie jar jammed full with bills.

Damn! I was surprised. I had no idea there was so much loose money aboard ship. The total crew complement at that time was fifty-one members not including the five officers.

Marcus continued, "Please show the players this list." He handed me a sheet of paper with an amount beside each name. "And give each named player his share of the lost loot. As house dealer playing against the five novices, I didn't deal a fair hand all night. What's more, not even the best of the players suspected I was crapping all over them."

Now I knew why many of the ship's company were so sullen.

Just before Marcus left the wardroom, he grinned at me and said, "Sir, I'll never skin them again, not the crew. I assure you. In addition, I'll keep my eyes peeled to see that games are kept under control."

The new cook interested me.

I called in the various players, chewed them out, showed them the list, and returned the money. They were dumbfounded. By the end of the day, the mood of the losers and their cohorts had changed one hundred eighty degrees. The crew held Marcus in high esteem. "He is one hell of a guy," was the universal theme. Following that episode, he was known by one and all on the 460.5 as "Cooky B."

When the ship headed for the southwest Pacific, one of my duties as the executive officer was to read and censor outgoing mail. For almost sixteen months, the correspondence by Cooky B to a girl in New York City named Mariana Lucas fascinated me because each letter to her was accompanied by a poem in his flowing handwriting. The poems, whether in rhyme, blank or free verse, were damned good—and many were romantic—sexy. I wondered from what work he was copying them, but never asked.

Marcus turned out to be a good cook, serving acceptable meals. There was a minimum of griping. However, always there was somebody who would bitch, but he never lost his composure.

At some time each day, when off duty, he went through a rigorous exercise routine; including push-ups, rope skipping and various muscle stretching activities. From the ship's bridge, I frequently watched him in the late afternoon as he worked out near the fantail. He was five-foot-eleven, sinuous, and his belly muscles rippled. Months later, after we journeyed to the southwest Pacific, I learned he had erected a small punching bag in one of the dry food storage rooms.

Cooky B frequently played penny ante poker with crewmembers and would delightfully dazzle them with sleight-of-hand card tricks, but he never again took advantage of "his guys." Though he was accepted as one of the boys, he wasn't, and most of the crew, including the officers, sensed Cooky B was someone different. That difference popped out at the damnedest times, in the most surprising ways. I often wondered if he ever realized how different he was from the rest of the ship's company. I doubt that he did.

One of three "unfit for sea duty" men put aboard the ship at Balboa, Panama, by the base personnel command was Jerry Vacinto, who turned out to be a problem, a dangerous drug addict. Shortly after the 460.5 left Panama and headed seaward, various members of the crew were unable to find their wallets, watches and a number of personal articles previously stowed in their bunk-side sea bags. On the third morning out of Balboa, Eugene Foyle, the pharmacist's mate discovered that his secure medicine cabinet, holding pain-suppressing drugs, had been broken into. Most of those drugs were gone. He was furious. Mutual distrust was spreading through the crew. Later that same day, Bos'n Mates Hatch and Maynard caught the bowery scum, Vascinto, in the act of stealing. He was high on drugs. They cornered him, but were leery of approaching the street-smart, out-of-control addict. He was wielding a rapier-like switchblade while threatening to disembowel both of them.

That evening, at a wardroom meeting concerning the incident, Hatch reported to me, "As if by magic, Cooky B arrived on the scene and quietly said, 'Stand aside. I can handle that little burned out bastard.'"

Hatch continued, "I never saw a man move more swiftly. He was like a mongoose snaring a cobra. One quick dart by him, the knife flew from Vascinto's hand and the out-of-control, little prick was screaming in agony as Cooky all but tore the druggy's arm from its socket." The crimes were solved and the lost items recovered. Vacinto was placed in a holding cell, constructed by crewmembers, until he was put ashore in Hollandia, New Guinea.

In July of 1945, before the war in the Pacific ended, Cooky B was granted a seven-day recreational leave by the Seventh Fleet Command. Though Bell, the yeoman, and I knew Cooky had applied for some kind of recreational break, neither of us knew why. A week after Cooky left on his leave, our ship was swinging at stern anchor in the Leyte Harbor, Philippines. I was standing by the ship's boarding ladder when a small boat pulled alongside, and Cooky B scrambled up the ladder, and came aboard with just a hint of a swagger. He had a mouse over his right eye. Under his left arm he carried a large blue velvet bag. When I inquired about it, he untied the drawstrings and pulled out a boxing trophy, with a jabbing male silver figurine on top of a square mahogany base. On one side of the base was a small silver plate inscribed "Marcus A. Bosconovich, Finalist, Middleweight Division, U.S. Navy, 7th Fleet, 27 July 1945." I was amazed. His comment was, "I had a hell of a good time. The guy that beat me had a right cross with the power of a mule kick."

Later that day, I talked with gunner's mate Henekin, and much to my surprise learned he had been a light-heavyweight club fighter. He had worked out with Cooky B in the dry food storage room that had the punching bag.

He said, "Cooky is one classy boxer. He learned to fight while at some school named Cornell and he won the Ivy League middleweight championship, whatever the hell the Ivy League is, won it at the Princeton Center, wherever in hell that is." He spoke of how his boxing shipmate could have won the fleet championship if he had more training and ring time. "But," said Henekin, "I am too old now to be of much help. I can't take the punchin'."

From Henekin's remarks, I surmised that Cooky B was a graduate of Cornell University. I never inquired of him about his background and he never offered. He apparently didn't want his true background known.

In November 1945, while the ship was anchored in the outer harbor of Inchon, Korea, I transferred command of the 460.5 to Norman Chesleski, my exec, and headed for home, Arlington, Virginia. Just before I boarded the Milwaukee Road Special in Seattle, Washington, bound for Chicago, I purchased three small paperback books to while away time as the train traveled east. After breakfast on the third day of my trip homeward, I returned to my Pullman seat and opened one of the three little paperback volumes. It was entitled *Poems by Three Pacific War Poets*. On the random page I had turned to was a poem, *The Mistress of Hell.* When I finished the first couple of lines, I knew I had read that poem before. For a few seconds I was bewildered, then remembered, I had read it, enclosed with a letter from Cooky B to Mariana, whoever she is. I thumbed to the table of contents and there, "Part 2, The Poems of Marcus Arent Bosconovich" I flipped the pages. A biographical sketch of the poet preceded the poems—before he entered the service. I read the brief bio with ever increasing interest. For the first time, I was truly introduced to my former shipmate. Mariana Finley Lucas wrote the vignette.

Marcus had been born in Chicago, Illinois. His father was of Russian descent, his mother was Italian. Marcus was blessed with a powerful body and brilliant mind. He had graduated from a Chicago high school with honors and won a scholarship to Cornell University. While there, he became a star member of the varsity boxing team. He graduated from Cornell with a double major; *math* and *English*. He remained at the university for an additional year to obtain his masters

115

degree in math. His Masters dissertation had been a writing entitled, *How to Gamble Right*. Marcus was apparently a blithe spirit. After college, he had been employed as a card dealer in a Reno casino. During his dealing days, he became interested in poetry, and started to seriously study the art.

Just prior to the United States entering World War II, Mariana Lucas, on vacation in Reno, met Marcus while he was working as a dealer at the casino. She was the young owner/publisher of The Purple Canary Press, a small, independent publishing house on 63rd Street off Lexington Avenue in New York City. She had encouraged the poetic efforts of Bosconovich and had included many of his poems in the volume published before the end of the war.

I gleaned from the vignette that Mariana and Marcus had become more than just friends. However, in early 1944, there appeared to have been a serious disagreement between the couple. Shortly thereafter, Bosconovich entered the U. S. Navy. She professed not to know where in the Pacific the young poet was serving his country. Even after their apparent spat, the couple continued to correspond and he had sent her his poems. She entered several in poetry contests. One of them had won a prestigious award. As evidenced by Mariana's writing, she had experienced a change of heart about Marcus. She was eagerly awaiting his return. Furthermore, she expressed the belief that he could have a successful career ahead of him as a poet and creative writer. I agreed with her, particularly after I had reread his poems. Most flowed with imagery, feeling, color and frequently with a hint of different interpretations. As I have said before, they were damned good.

There now was no doubt in my mind that Cooky B was not only an intriguing guy, but was talented in many ways. I resolved to keep in contact with him. That resolution was easier made than kept. Time and again, despite my efforts, I lost track of him. What follows is, to my knowledge, the real account of his life, after he left L.S.M. 460.5 and through the date of this writing. Marcus Bosconovich, my friend, is truly one lucky guy.

Gregory T. Morgan
Former Senior Lieutenant U. S.
Naval Reserve,
and former Commanding Officer of
the U.S.S.
L.S.M. 460.5

CLARITY
BY
LINDA ADAMS

Linda Adams was born and raised in Southern California, amidst a collection of dogs, cats, and people with strange personalities. She started writing short stories when she was eight, with the goal of eventually writing a novel. It was a big goal that took a while to accomplish. In the meantime, she enlisted in the Army, serving nine years that took her to the unexpected—the first war in the Persian Gulf. She eventually ended up in Northern Virginia with a collection of teddy bears with strange personalities and a "Wascally Wesident Wabbit" for a co-writer, Emory Hackman. Linda and Emory (known as Hackman-Adams) are co-writing a pursuit thriller for women set in the Shenandoah Valley during the Civil War. Linda has been published in the anthology *Nudges From God*, as well as *The Toastmaster, Potomac Review, The Plaza, _Mocha Memoirs,* and *The Writers' Journal*. She is a member of Washington Independent Writers, the nation's largest writers' trade association. Please visit her Web site at **http://www.hackman-adams.com**.

Then a name caught my eye. A single name. It was not a familiar name, but I recognized it.

CLARITY
By
Linda Adams

Non-Fiction

Desert Storm was now falling distantly behind me. But with the distance, the veneer I didn't know I had put up was dissolving. Suddenly things I'd carefully hidden away were coming out and demanding attention.

I didn't know what to do. Those who had been in the war were in a happy state of denial, and those who hadn't been were mired in bureaucracy. I was left alone in my thoughts, feeling that no one understood. Nor even cared.

That day, I'd come up to see the marble grandiosity of the state capital. But somehow, my feet found the curving sidewalk that went between the trees. Abruptly, I stepped into the brightness of open sky and saw what was at the end of the path.

The Wall.

I felt drawn to it. As I stepped across the line etched in the sidewalk that completed the circle of the Wall, a cloud of silence descended over me. No birds chirped, no airplanes flew overhead. Absolute silence.

I looked at the panels with the columns of names. I didn't know any of them, but I knew every one of them.

And they knew me. I was one of them.

My fingers trailed along the names. All that was left of them was etched in stone. But I could feel them all, watching me, silently now, to see what I would do.

Then a name caught my eye. A single name. It was not a familiar name, but I recognized it.

My fingers trembled as they touched the name, feeling the hard edges.

A woman.

She'd been at war.

Like me.

She had no voice. But I could hear her clearly. And she could hear me—all of me! The good, the bad, the hurt, the anger, everything that we shared.

It was enough. I suddenly didn't feel so alone any more.

A SOLDIER'S FORTUNE
BY
MARIE A. ROY

Marie A. Roy was born June 11, 1946 in Hartford, Connecticut where she lived with her parents and twin sister. At age four she and her family moved to Rocky Hill, Connecticut where she would develop a love for fiction writing. In 1969 she married Robert G. Roy, a dedicated high school math teacher. They moved to Terryville, Connecticut where they raised two sons, both now married each with two children of their own.

Marie dedicates her portion of this book to her late husband Robert G. Roy, who after having taught 34 years, died July 6, 2002 at the age of 55. She also dedicates this book to her father, Louis A. Visone, a WWII veteran who at the age of 88 died on June 13, 2003. Marie currently does volunteer work within the Hospice Program at a local hospital. She is currently working on a non-fiction book on widowhood, dating and relationships. She has also completed a romantic mystery suspense novel. Marie has had two romances published, *A Soldier's Fortune*, which can be found at **www.trebleheartbooks.com.** *No More Secrets, No More Lies,* though currently still in print is unavailable at the moment.

Lia repeated the name silently. Russell Scott McIntyre had fought a war where more than thirty years later no one could say who the actual winners were.

A SOLDIER'S FORTUNE
By
Marie A. Roy

Fiction

Reprinted with permission by Treble Heart Books

EPILOGUE

A Year Later—November

Skeletal branches arched up toward a steely sky. Lia knew beneath the cold ground, seeds of continuing life would eventually produce the promised flowers of spring. A crisp breeze blew through her mid-length hair.

On either side of her stood five figures reflected by a ribbon of dark granite. Her eyes panned the glossy surface. So many names, she thought, far too many names.

Shivers ran through her, caused not by the cold but from something else that stirred deep inside. On her right, Pop sat in a wheelchair. In his uncertainty, he kept his hands folded in his lap. The protective lambskin collar of his thick green corduroy jacket was pulled up to his ears. He hadn't spoken much since leaving the hotel.

Sean stood on her left. He also hadn't said much since getting up that morning. Now lost in thought, dressed in jeans, a dark brown bomber jacket, he kept close to her side. Unsure of what to do with his own hands, he awkwardly held a charcoal pencil and paper that had been given to him by the local park attendant.

"Here's the panel," Harry whispered, reverently.

"Yeah, now we just have to look for the line," Sean replied.

Lia held her breath, feeling a rush of anticipation surge through. She glanced at Brad. A younger version of his father, his face showing curiosity, confusion and something else she couldn't quite discern. Brad turned, met his mother's gaze. "I'm a generation from this," he quietly commented.

Lia nodded, forcing down a fear and the image of having to search the Wall for her son's name, instead of the name of a dead brother-in-law.

"There it is," Harry pointed out, drawing close to the reflective surface. His voice was soft, respectfully remorseful.

Sean drew in a breath, joined Harry and for a long moment studied the inscription. Resignedly, as if finally able to accept the truth about his brother, he lifted the pencil and pressed it firmly against the unyielding surface then rubbed across the paper with the pencil. Through

120

broad even strokes, dark slate letters emerged.

RUSSELL SCOTT MCINTYRE.

Lia repeated the name silently. Russell Scott McIntyre had fought a war where more than thirty years later no one could say who the actual winners were.

She felt a delicate whisper-like touch pressing into her palm. Comfort followed as Tuyet's fingers intertwined with hers.

Soft murmurs drifted from the other visitors who lives had in some way become entangled in a similar pain, a similar resignation, and a similar acceptance that allowed them to eventually heal.

Suddenly, Eliah pushed himself up out of his wheelchair, and approached the Wall. From one pocket, he drew an object. Lia, at first could not make it out except that it had been wrapped in plain white tissue paper.

As Eliah unfolded the mysterious package, she saw that they were some of his prized arrowheads, ones he had treasured for more years than she could remember. Then he drew from his other pocket a string of beads, the only finds to originate from the rescue dig, which although some would regard as unsuccessful as far as finding tangible treasures, they all had found so much more—each other.

To give himself support, Eliah placed one hand below the letters of Russell's name, and then eased himself down toward the ground where he placed his offering of arrowheads and beads.

Sean watched, said nothing. After a moment, he placed a hand beneath Eliah's elbow, and helped him back to his feet.

Lia, Tuyet, Harry, and Brad moved toward the two men, forming a semi-circle of comfort.

They had all been there in Vietnam, Lia felt, in some manner. She traced the letters of her brother-in-law's name.

How strange, she thought. Cold in appearance, yet it felt warm to the touch. She stared at the cross pattern, which had once declared Russell an MIA. She traced the diamond shaped lines that had been etched there a year later, confirming his death.

Sean's hand covered hers, and then drew it away from the stone surface. Lovingly, he looked at her. She met his gaze, and felt grateful for the life that now stretched before them as well as the memories that would eventually heal all wounds.

I FEEL SO FREE
BY
BETTE MILLESON JAMES

Bette Milleson James, a niece/sister/cousin of many family veterans, is a Kansas writer and award-winning teacher of English language arts and technology. She served her school district as grant writer and later wrote original poetry and did research on classic writers for artist N.A. Noel's book, *I Am Wherever You Are*. She also has publication credits in two anthologies, *Let Us Not Forget*, from iUniverse, and *Forget Me Knots...From the Front Porch*, published by Obadiah Press. She and her husband raised three children on a wheat, corn, and livestock farm west of Hoxie Kansas, where they still live, and where she writes daily.

Etched into my memory forever is a picture of the father—whose home in Guatemala is surrounded by a ten-foot solid stone wall with barbed wire rolled along the top—standing on the grass in front of our house, looking at the stars and raising his arms into the wind, saying, "This is paradise. I feel so free!"

I FEEL SO FREE
By
Bette Milleson James

Non-Fiction

I stood alone in the shelter of a long, covered porch at the front of our country home as a thunderstorm raged on an evening that had changed suddenly, in typical Kansas fashion, from mellow moonlight to lightning-crossed brilliance. In the distance, I saw the lights of our small town come and go as the flashes obliterated and the darkness redeemed their sparkle. Out there in the damp windy air, I thought of other porches, other storms, other times, and all the homes where these things have been a part of my life.

In our part of the Midwest, the far western ends of Nebraska and Kansas, rain is scarce enough to be celebrated no matter how it comes. It is important and noteworthy, and I have always been unable to take it for granted. As a child, I played rainy day tag with my brothers and the neighbor children on the front porch of a concrete-block duplex where we lived in North Platte, Nebraska, during the 'forties. Sometimes the moms made popcorn or fudge, and often the games settled into story times or playing "house" or "school." The old porch seemed a big place to me then, as many places do when we are children. On returning years later, I found a rather small house with a covered concrete porch along one side, and standing there in the yard among old lilac bushes and cottonwood trees, I felt those early days all around me.

World War Two was raging when we lived in the duplex, and we had, right there in unlikely Nebraska, air-raid drills and "blackouts." At designated times, all over town, the mothers turned out all but the dimmest lights and pulled down the "blackout shades," the city officials and businesses darkened street lights and neon signs, and the cars pulled over, lights out. We all went outside and waited under the stars for the airplanes from the base at Omaha to fly over, looking for lights on earth from the night sky above. I had no idea of the purpose then, but I remember being lifted up by my father as we waited, and watching the lights of airplanes moving steadily among the stars. Afterward, children and parents sat on the porch or on the block steps talking quietly in an eerie darkness, and I felt somehow safe and permanent. It seemed no more unusual an event to me than Mother's making big trays of sandwiches to take to the Union Pacific Depot, where Red Cross volunteers maintained a coffee-and-sandwich canteen for soldiers who passed through constantly on troop trains that whistled from time to time both day and night and spoke to me of faraway places.

Many years later, describing this, a young man in a college class told me indignantly that there were air raid blackouts only on the two coasts. But my hometown is a railroad town, with a large installation there, and the railroads, absolutely essential for the movement of troops across the country, were considered to be at risk. I knew I was right, and I still cherish the memory of those dark and quiet nights, when someone very wise seemed to be hovering over us.

Time moved on in my life, and letters were sent by a soldier brother and a cousin from France, from Korea, in time from Army bases and diplomatic posts all over the world. Through the years, a series of dorm rooms and apartments finally gave way to another small house with a covered front porch. Like my mother, I couldn't resist being outside on the porch when it rained, especially with thunder and lightning. My own children, grown and gone, have their memories now of wrapping up in an afghan in a chair on that little porch, of popcorn or fudge, of books and storytelling, of sometimes just watching the rain as it fell. I see their small figures, cuddled in their blankets in a chilly spring, or running into the rain and back to the porch on warm summer days, splashing and giggling at the change in routine brought by weather. Their innocence was unaware that another war was raging, an uncle gone to Vietnam, and it seemed to me that time was revolving and renewing old experiences both tragic and true.

In those days, there were toys on the porch, of course, a wagon, a tricycle, a very important rocking horse with squeaky springs. Our middle child so loved that horse that she rocked long and contentedly every day, inevitably growing sleepy. When the squeak of the springs slowed down, I dropped whatever I was doing and went to the porch, where a sleepy two-year-old was beginning to sway ominously on the back of her pony. She never once awoke when I caught her limp little body and carried her off to bed.

A few years later, home was an old Victorian farmhouse with wraparound porches front and back. Older and more sophisticated, the children didn't cuddle much on the porch any more, though they still loved the novelty of rain and thunderstorms and would sometimes drag a rocking chair outside to watch the weather. Mainly, those porches were home to numerous pets on the farm, a dog always, sometimes two, and large, longhaired gray cats with inevitable litters of kittens brought up from the barn to the porch. We still have photos of Tippy, sleeping by the back door with four or five kittens on top of him, warming their paws and noses in the big dog's thick coat of winter fur.

Eventually, we made a final move to a new house with the essential big front porch, this time of brick, with arches defining the front and wide eaves giving added protection from the weather. It is there that I go now to watch the flashes of distant lightning and hear the rolling of thunder that seems to come from every direction, as I have done for more than twenty-five years. It is there that our family finished growing up and prepared to leave home, there that we went at times to escape the noise or activity in the house, there that we grew to share confidences and problems and to seek solutions. In the quiet shelter of the porch, I sat uncounted times waiting for a teenaged son to come home, for some critical piece of mail to arrive, for carloads of friends or family or returning college students to drive into the yard.

One summer, our eighth-grade daughter wanted desperately to go to a particular dance in town. We sat sadly on the front porch, seeing the lights in the distance—she, wishing she could go, and I, wishing the dance were appropriate for her. Somehow the front porch kept us centered, and held at bay the feelings of anger that can arise when "No" is the only possible answer.

On a more recent summer day, we welcomed visitors from Central America, members of a family we have known for many years. After a celebratory meal, the crowd of people naturally gravitated to the front porch and spilled over onto the lawn. Etched into my memory forever is a picture of the father—whose home in Guatemala is surrounded by a ten-foot solid stone wall with barbed wire rolled along the top—standing on the grass in front of our house, looking at the stars and raising his arms into the wind, saying, "This is paradise. I feel so free!" A gentle man from a distant and difficult land, he redefined "home" more broadly for me—as a house, a country, a state of the heart and a gift from the past. How I loved home that day.

Now the front porch is frequented by grandchildren, who love the red glider seat and the wide yard, which cuddle into a blanket when it rains and believe that their popcorn and snacks and stories are necessary parts of a rainy day. For their mother, the porch is part of the identity of "home," and when she seems to have disappeared that is where we find her.

Somehow those early experiences of popcorn and candy-making, of lilacs and cottonwoods, of books and comfort and safety have defined my life and extended to those of my descendants, as, I suppose, our early experiences always do. We cannot escape ourselves, nor can our children escape our influences. Time out of mind, old generations have lived on through young ones, and in our family we tend to realize who we are and to nurture the traditions that have helped us to prevail. Now, I sit on the porch in summer and remember the darkened streets of the war years and the great gift of freedom those years bought so dearly for us all. I see again the little house in the rain, the wraparound porch of later years, the wide brick arches defining the flashes of light and the wind-tossed trees in the distance. I remember once more the words of our friend whose life is so different from ours, and I know that his truth is also mine: "This is paradise. I feel so free."

ETERNAL COMRADE
BY
STEVEN MANCHESTER

The father of two sons and one beautiful, little girl, Steven Manchester is the published author of *The Unexpected Storm: The Gulf War Legacy, Jacob Evans, A Father's Love, Warp II* and *At The Stroke of Midnight*, as well as several books under the pseudonym, Steven Herberts. His work has been showcased in such national literary journals as *Taproot Literary Review, American Poetry Review* and *Fresh! Literary Magazine.* Steven is an accomplished speaker, and currently teaches the popular workshop "Write A Book, Get Published & Promote Your Work". Three of his screenplays have also been produced as films. When not spending time with his children, writing, teaching, or promoting his published books/films, this Massachusetts author speaks publicly to troubled children through the "Straight Ahead" Program. See: **http://www.StevenManchester.com**.

Men like you and me were forced to learn that- not all war wounds are visible, nor are they all suffered on the battlefield.

ETERNAL COMRADE
By
Steven Manchester

Non-Fiction

Dear Marc,

It's hard to believe, brother, but it's been ten years since we served side-by-side in Operation Desert Storm, As U.S. Army M.P.'s in Iraq, we shared every trying experience one could imagine during war. They labeled us the *Dream Team,* though as you know, our experience was anything but a dream. I've learned that our perspective of the Gulf War is very different from the sanitized version CNN opted to show. I'm sure few people know of the children- we witnessed- get slaughter by land mines. I'm also sure that few people know anything about such hefty costs associated with freedom. I envy them. And, I also wish we could have talked about the pain.

During the 100 hours of ground fighting in the Middle East, there were so many friends that we made and lost, so many battles waged on an internal front, and so many promises that were broken from those who sent us. Though we returned home visibly whole, what we brought with us as a result of experimental vaccines, radioactive depleted uranium, and pent-up rage is more than any man should be asked to carry. "It's a just cause," they said, "Babies are being tossed from hospital incubators in Kuwait." I still wish our government saw our cause to be equally just.

When we got home, I know that you suffered from PTSD, with nightmares, flashbacks, depression, and terrible insomnia. Your Mom also told me that you had severe headaches, joint pain, liver problems, respiratory problems, digestive problems, undiagnosed lump on his chest. But, the VA told you that your problems weren't service-connected, therefore, they couldn't really help you. It's criminal, I know! I was given the same answers.

I guess we were taught to value loyalty above all things except honor, while those who called us to serve didn't have to show either?

But the physical pain is only a fraction of it, isn't it? Men like you and me were forced to learn that- not all war wounds are visible, nor are they all suffered on the battlefield. We also learned that war is a state of mind and that a man cannot live in two worlds at one time. Eventually, there has to be a truce! I wish, more than anything, I could have helped you find that truce.

I sensed that you had a tough time trying to heal. You were one of the lucky few who'd tried everything to patch up some of the Iraqi kids that never made it. I imagine that gory picture haunted you for years. It's certainly haunted me.

For reasons that reach beyond mercy, upon our return though, the *Dream Team* parted ways and we only saw each other at special events. The best explanation I have for this is that it actually became less painful to avoid faces that served as reminders of a difficult time (no matter how much we loved the people behind the faces).

Marc, trust me, you were never alone in your struggle, and this is the greatest tragedy to come out of Operation Desert Storm. Not one of us had to suffer alone. Yet, that's all any of us have done for a decade.

I learned this far too late, but you eventually turned to drugs and got hooked bad. It brought relief from your demons, I'm sure. I'm also sure that you fought desperately for years to beat those demons back. They told me that your son was only five when those demons finally won. Your Mom said that you died at home with her right by your side. Although it was a horrific scene, she said she was so glad she was there with you—even though she couldn't save you. When I heard this, I wept like a child. But I was also relieved that you didn't die alone. I am eternally grateful that you passed over with someone who really loved you by your side. Now, I can only pray that this incredible tragedy has finally brought you peace from your demons.

I'm writing you now to let you know that I haven't forgotten: When we were in the Gulf, you were there for me when I really needed help. I've always felt I owed you one (though I'm sure you'd argued that). In any event, as I never got the chance to pay you back, I now owe it to your son, Anthony. I don't know that I'll be able to clear my debt until Anthony gets older, but it's my word that on the day he really needs someone, I'll be there. His honorable father already paid for it!

This past Veterans Day, the *Dream Team* (12 of us) went to the cemetery and had a remembrance at your gravesite that lasted better than two hours. The beer was cold and it was quite emotional, though I'm confident you already know these things.

While the boys and me were at the cemetery, a stranger approached with his mentally retarded son. Their presence felt peculiar. The man prayed at the stone to the left of yours, and then walked over to ask what you died from. I hurried to explain that you'd been sick from the Gulf, and that...when Doug Donnoly interrupted, saying, "He died of a broken heart." It was as good an explanation as any, so I nodded. The stranger smiled and said he understood, and then walked away with his boy. At first, I didn't think much of it. On the way home, though, I started to question whether or not it was a coincidence.

I promise that Anthony will know that his Dad was a great man, and loved by many men who also chose to serve a purpose higher than themselves. 'Goombah,' you were loved very much, and still are! And, you are still quite respected by people who don't show respect unless it is earned. I miss you terribly, brother, but have also experienced enough to know in my heart that it's only a brief matter of time before we reunite and laugh over old times.

I recently wrote the American Gulf War Veterans Association for you and Anthony. I told them that I have a comrade from the war that died; that he was ill for many years and could not find relief at the VA. As a result, he self-medicated himself until he silenced his pain with an overdose. His name was Marc Susi (Sgt.) and he was a very honorable man: one hell of a soldier. Tragically, he left behind an 8-year old son named Anthony. And although my brothers from the *Dream Team* and I will insure that the boy knows his Dad was an honorable man, we could use some help. I told them that I fear that Anthony may grow up thinking that his Dad's premature death was the result of some random addiction and not the result of war. I explained that this boy should take pride in his Dad's service to America in ODS. I told them that you were one of the few heroes I've ever met, and that you would have given your own soul to a dying Iraqi child. I told them everything.

One month later, Anthony received a medal in the mail. The letter attached said that he was being awarded the medal for his sacrifice toward the liberation of Kuwait. I know you're proud.

Brother, trust that when the time is right, I will tell your son: Your father's death was not caused by some random addiction. He was a casualty of war. And because of his premature death, you have also been forced to sacrifice a great deal for the liberation of Kuwait. You are one of us now. Do not be haunted by silence. Be proud of what your father gave to his country, and understand it was that noble decision which took his life. If anyone questions who your father was, you have thirty "uncles" that you can call on to help you explain. I'd be insulted if you didn't! Be proud, Anthony, and always keep your chin up. Your Dad was a bonafide hero!"

I love you, brother. I'll be seeing you soon.

Your eternal comrade,

Steve Manchester

WAR AND FAMILIES
BY
RAE SHAPIRO

Rae Shapiro has turned to writing as a second career after thirty years teaching preschoolers and their parents. During this time she also raised two children, earned a B. A. in English and an M. A. in Early Childhood Education. Besides the schoolwork, there was always writing for professional newsletters along the way.

In 1990 she retired from teaching, and took the time to see the world with her husband Julius. In 1998 she got a computer and changed the direction of her life. Since then she took a second prize at the Houston Writers' Conference in March of 2000, and saw her words in print in an anthology put together by Barbara Delinsky called *Uplift* (October 2001). All proceeds go to breast cancer research. She also contributed an essay to *Crumbs in the Keyboard: Women Who Juggle Life and Writing*, an anthology that will support women's shelters. (June 2002)

She also has been published several times in the Vintage Villager, a senior magazine. Two of her articles were included in recent issues of LARA Confidential, the newsletter of Los Angeles Romance Authors, a Chapter of RWA...Romance Writers of America. She is working on two novels and several short stories.

She lives in Van Nuys, California with her husband of forty-nine years, and three cats who adopted them.

When Albert was reported missing in action, and then dead, Aunt Lena wrote to President Roosevelt. She wanted her surviving son sent home. The answer? If you have two sons killed in action, we will send home the third. Unfortunately, there were just the two.

WAR AND FAMILIES
By
Rae Shapiro

Non-Fiction

This story begins with my Maternal Grandmother's family. She was one of six sisters: Sarah, (my grandmother), Lena, Bertha, Hannah, Ida, and Esther. They all married, and with the exception of Lena, had daughters. All of those cousins are gone now, with the exception of Pearl, my mother's sister, and my cousin Golda. They are both in their eighties. Golda is in great shape—Pearl is not.

In December 2001, Aunt Pearl went into the hospital. She had been living with her husband, my Uncle Joe, who is blind, diabetic, and suffers from periodic bouts of congestive heart failure. They had, of their own volition, moved into a retirement hotel about five years before. My sister and I assessed the situation, and decided it was time for a change, preferably to a group home for assisted living. We got Uncle Joe into a lovely place. Auntie was still in the hospital. Now the real work began.

We had to close out their apartment and sift through sixty years of memorabilia. It was a monumental job. While I was going through their papers, I came across many items that stirred my memories. Clipped together were two newspaper pictures: one was of my daughter and her Girl Scout troop mates, showing how they had earned a badge for needlework. That daughter now has two girl scouts of her own, continuing into a third generation of Girl Scout leadership...my mother, myself, and now my daughter. But the picture that caused the greatest flood of memories was of my cousin Albert, in his Air Force uniform, telling of his death over St. Lo in France. He and his brother, Cousin Jerry, were the two male cousins of that generation, my Aunt Lena's boys.

Albert was the one that was married. I had been at his wedding. I'm sure I attended the ceremony with my parents, but it was the rest of the day that was so memorable for me, and the reason I was able to place the time accurately.

Aunt Pearl and Uncle Joe, being childless, always had special feelings for my sister and me. That day, they took me to see the movie *Best Foot Forward*, with Lucille Ball. I looked it up in a dictionary of movie stars. It was a 1943 release. It was what I would call a "Rah Rah" story, about winning at football. Looking back, I think it was probably a metaphor for winning the war. In it, there was a song I remember:

"Buckle down Winsockie, buckle down.
You can win, Winsockie if you buckle down.
You can win, Winsockie, you can win, Winsockie,
You can win, Winsockie, if you buckle, buckle down."

    I could sing that song right now, fifty-nine years later. Aunt Pearl and Uncle Joe made many of my days memorable like that one. Two years before, I had been a flower girl in their wedding. They are closely entwined in my life.

    When Albert was reported missing in action, and then dead, Aunt Lena wrote to President Roosevelt. She wanted her surviving son sent home. The answer? If you have two sons killed in action, we will send home the third. Unfortunately, there were just the two. The little article says Cousin Albert was a bomber engineer on a B-24 Liberator. We always called him a bombardier. Being only the second son, Cousin Jerry's life was forfeit over the English Channel. He was a tail gunner. How many war stories have filmed scenes showing men dying in those positions— too many to count, just like the reality.

    I always remembered Aunt Lena and Uncle Sam as sad people. When the war ended, they retired to Florida, on what they called their "blood money"...the proceeds from their sons' GI insurance. They lived quietly, doing good works: driving blind veterans to and from appointments, and reading to them. They died quietly the way they lived, at a much younger age than the rest of the siblings.

DESERT BOOMERANG
BY
STEVEN MANCHESTER

The father of two sons and one beautiful, little girl, Steven Manchester is the published author of *The Unexpected Storm: The Gulf War Legacy, Jacob Evans, A Father's Love, Warp II* and *At The Stroke of Midnight,* as well as several books under the pseudonym, Steven Herberts. His work has been showcased in such national literary journals as *Taproot Literary Review, American Poetry Review* and *Fresh! Literary Magazine.* Steven is an accomplished speaker, and currently teaches the popular workshop "Write A Book, Get Published & Promote Your Work". Three of his screenplays have also been produced as films. When not spending time with his children, writing, teaching, or promoting his published books/films, this Massachusetts author speaks publicly to troubled children through the "Straight Ahead" Program. See: **http://www.StevenManchester.com**.

I watched my entire life unfold before me. I was euphoric. I was at peace. Then, as if reality was given its last chance, I thought, All of this, only to die in a Hum-V accident?

DESERT BOOMERANG
By
Steven Manchester

Non-Fiction

In 1991, as a shield was replaced by an angry storm, Saddam Hussein threatened America with the mother of all battles. In turn, President George Bush drew a line in the sand. That line was quickly wrapped around Iraq and used to choke the life out of thousands. As a U.S. Army M.P., I was there when the Americans crossed the breach from Saudi Arabia into Iraq, crushing the first of three Iraqi lines of defense along the way. It was like someone had lifted the curtain to Hell, giving everyone a free peek. It was Hell on earth.

It took four days, or a mere 100 hours, before the ground war was ceased. History was made. In triumph, Kuwait was liberated, while Hussein was humiliated before the whole world. An unconditional withdrawal was ordered. Politically, the sadistic demon was slain. In reality, unlike thousands of his own people, he still lived. Yet, with my introduction to the "Mystery Illness," the war was far from over.

Two weeks after the last shot was fired, I was standing at a barren traffic control point in Iraq when a lone vehicle approached. It was American, so I waved it through. The driver pulled up to me and stopped. He was a black sergeant and from the look in his eyes, he was definitely lost.

"Man, am I glad to see you!" he said with a nervous grin. "I lost my convoy in the dust storm that just passed through. I'm supposed to be on Main Supply Route Green, but..."

I chuckled. The entire area was my patrol, and I could have driven the roads in Iraq blindly. "You're not that far off," I confirmed. "Right now, you're on M.S.R. Blue, but this route runs parallel to M.S.R. Green. Keep south for the next four miles or so, and when you reach a fork in the road, you've met up with Green."

The sergeant's face showed relief, and I was happy to help him. With a wave, he was on his way. I, on the other hand, returned to the boredom of the desert's miles and miles of solitary confinement.

Several very unpleasant months passed. One afternoon, in base camp, my platoon sergeant, Tony Rosini, approached. "Hey kid, got any plans today?"

"Yeah, I think I'll head to the mall," I joked.

He chuckled. "In that case, you can give me a ride into Saudi Arabia. My knee's been acting up, so maybe they'll give me some painkillers. Either way, I could use the time away and from the look of it, so could you."

My arm felt the twist. "Whose vehicle?" I asked.

Tony never answered. He just slid into the passenger seat of his own. A Horse With No Name.

We were making good time and traveled down the dusty road at a fast clip. We joked and laughed, with only 40 miles between the Saudi Arabian border and us. Before long, the radio traffic ceased. We were out of range. I noticed our vehicle had been the only vehicle on the road since we left. I continued to scan the vast terrain to insure we were alone. Some of the Republican Guard was still on the loose, soldiers who came out of hiding during the dark hours. The farther we drove, though, the less it mattered. We were nearly an hour from safety.

Several miles later, I slowed down. We'd hit a dust storm, a bad one. I could hardly see three feet past the windshield. In the blink of an eye, the blue sky turned a blinding orange, as the harsh winds of the open desert rearranged the landscape. With the help of hurricane winds, tons of sand leapt into the atmosphere and decided to fly around for a while. Maneuvering the Hum-V right and left, I slowed down even more. The snake-shaped trail offered sharper corners. Squinting, I concentrated and drove on.

Then the nightmare began.

Approximately 30 miles from the border, I heard the bang. Unaware of the cause, it was a loud crash that came from the right side of the vehicle. The cause didn't matter, because the rest was out of my hands.

In super slow motion, the vehicle tipped left toward the driver's side. The windshield cracked at the top, then spidered throughout the center. As amazement swam within my eyes, the desert spun in circles, end-over-end. I felt something heavy smash into the back of my bare skull. It was an army field phone, flying around aimlessly, until it found its target. The piercing pain quickly led to numbness. My tense body went limp. I felt as if I were being submerged into a pool of warm water. Unlike any peace I experienced before, the sensation was heavenly. With no choice but to accept the comfort, my eyes slammed shut. In the briefest moment in time, I watched as my life played out before me. It was a slide show, with one vivid picture after another being brought to light.

I watched my entire life unfold before me. I was euphoric. I was at peace. Then, as if reality was given its last chance, I thought, *All of this, only to die in a Hum-V accident?* I fought it off with everything inside of me. I didn't want death. It wasn't my time. I fought, but the struggle was brief. There was no more pain, no more peace, and no more pictures. There was only darkness.

I opened my eyes and felt a methodical pain surge throughout my body. My entire body throbbed, but it was my left arm and neck that caused me to groan. Attempting to lift my heavy head, my mind twirled in circles, fogged from the pain and disoriented from the shock. Turning my head slowly, I looked down at my fingers. The only thing missing was my wedding band. Turning right, I saw the Hum-V. It was almost 40 feet away, lying on its roof. It looked funny, like a helpless turtle resting on its shell. Reality struck. It wasn't at all funny. With all my might, I pushed to my knees. The Hum-V's motor screamed for help. It was running at full idle. Trying to clear my blurred vision, I choked on the smell of gas and oil that leaked from the wreck. I took two small, painful steps toward the Hum-V when I saw him. It was Tony.

Like a bat, my platoon sergeant hung upside down within the wreckage. He was suspended in mid-air by a seat belt and appeared unconscious. My heart jumped into my throat and started beating wildly. Tony was in trouble. He needed help. Picking up the pace, I ignored my own pain. "Get out! Tony, get out!" I screamed.

Tony never moved, but the motor seemed to hear me. It raced faster. Without hesitation, I dove into the Hum-V.

I was right. Tony was out cold. Instinctively, I unbuckled the safety belt and awkwardly pulled my friend out. It was dead weight, but I continued to drag him, hoping that I wasn't causing more damage. There was no way to tell if Tony broke his back or neck. Then, I realized that I wasn't even sure whether Tony was even alive. I dragged faster.

A safe distance from the Hum-V, I laid Tony onto the warm sand and took his pulse. The old horse was still kicking. Feeling the greatest sense of relief, I was promptly reacquainted with my own pain. The intensity made me nauseous. I felt as if I were going to pass out, but fought it off. Though I wanted nothing more, there was no time for a nap. Tony was coming out of it.

For a while, I just sat in the sand, with Tony's head in my lap. The motor finally seized up. Tony talked in riddles. His gibberish told me that he was in shock. So, as the army trained me, I treated the symptoms accordingly.

I loosened the man's restrictive clothing and elevated his feet. I moistened Tony's lips with water. Bending over, I shaded my platoon sergeant's face from the sun's burning fingers. Unsure whether he could understand or not, I also began reassuring my friend. It was the biggest act of my life, but I promised, "Don't you worry, Tony. I'll get us out of this one. We'll be O.K." The empty words drifted off into the lonely desert. I was overcome with guilt. "My God, Tony, what have I done?" I whispered.

Tony never answered. He just mumbled and shivered from the cold. The shiver scared me. It was more than 90 degrees, and my friend was freezing. Removing my shirt, I covered my platoon sergeant's upper body, and then headed back to the smashed Hum-V. I needed to figure out a plan.

The closer I got, the more I could understand. The plan would be difficult, but our dilemma was easy enough to solve. It was an accident.

In the midst of the heavy dust storm, we hit a boulder with the right front tire. The Hum-V flipped three or four times, completely crushing the driver's side. It finally landed on its roof. The driver's side door was lying 20 feet from the scene. My spine tingled when I saw it.

It was too bizarre to be coincidental. I wasn't wearing a helmet, which allowed the telephone to knock me out. In turn, my body was thrown around at will. My seat belt would have trapped me under the weight of the wreckage, but that was never a problem. I forgot to put it on. The door flew off, throwing me out of the truck and away from the final landing. That was the clincher. If each factor didn't happen, in sequence, I would have been smashed like a grape. For reasons unknown to me, I was still alive. It was no less than a miracle. From then on, I felt as if I were on borrowed time. I didn't like the feeling.

Searching the ruined interior of the totaled wreck, my suffering mind was consumed with worry. We were in the middle of nowhere, with nothing but sand in all directions. There was no food and maybe enough water for six hours under the relentless sun. Worse of all, there was no communications! The antenna was buried under the wreck and though I tried again-and-again, it was no use. Nobody heard my pleas for help. Nobody knew we existed. Even the boys back at base camp didn't expect us back for a whole day. There would be no search for at least that long. A helpless fear welled up inside of me. Like a stranded child searching for his parents, I called for a medi-vac one last time. I waited. There was a terrible silence. With the antenna buried under the Hum-V, no one could have ever heard my beckoning. We were alone! Fighting off despair, I grabbed my rifle, a box of ammo and a ragged blanket, and returned to Tony. The only thing left was faith. Somewhere along the line, I was blinded. For me, there was no hope in sight.

Tony became more coherent and asked, "What the hell happened?"

I explained the accident, adding an apology at the end.

Tony raised his hands toward the sky. "You worry too much Stevie-boy. Just get us the hell out of here!"

I smiled, and then lied straight into my friend's frightened eyes. "No sweat boss. I made the call. Help should be here in no time."

Tony said nothing. He just grinned weakly and returned to unconsciousness.

Rocking him back and forth, I looked over at the wreck. The hopelessness tore at my very core. Looking down at my older friend, I knew it was better that Tony didn't know the truth: a truth that meant probable death. There was nothing I could do. WE were both in rough shape. Traveling on foot was impossible. The radio was no longer an option. The only thing to do was wait. I hated that lack of control. As the steady breezes covered Tony and me with sand, I felt as if we were sitting in an hourglass with our time running out. With all Allied forces heading farther north, the chances of someone driving past were very slim. Sitting somewhere on the southern tip of Iraq, under a drift of powdered sugar, we were in big trouble.

The two longest hours of my life passed without a change in our dilemma. With each passing minute, the outcome looked more bleak. Tony was in-and-out of consciousness, unaware of time and most other things. I sat alone, wincing from my physical pain and struggling with the mental torment. It was too much. My platoon sergeant was getting worse and there was nothing more I could do. The trauma tore me apart, piece-by-piece. I feared Tony's death more than my own and was already carrying the guilt for both. For the first time during the war, I cried.

Time crawled by, though it was irrelevant. Tony was dying from his physical wounds, and I was all but dead inside. I continued to console my trusting friend, while compassionately stroking what little hair was left. Tony spoke in riddles, babbling every once in awhile.

Like an infant, I sat deserted, stranded in the wild. I'd never felt so broken and alone. Tony was there, but only in the physical sense. I sobbed in guilt, despair, even self-pity. I never wanted to die alone. Then, without even realizing it, I didn't have to. The cavalry was on its way. Some true Americans appeared on the horizon. A miracle had been sent.

The hand of an angel rested on my shoulder. Looking up, I stared into the face of the blackest man I ever saw. The soldier bent down and gently whispered, "Lay down, Sarge. I'm gonna take care of you now. It's all over. We're gonna get you out of here." With that, he winked.

I couldn't believe it. It was the lost soldier I'd directed a few months before.

"But how did you..." I started.

He smiled. "Nice to see you again, too. After the directions you gave me, I finally found my medical unit." He looked back at the road. "I've been assigned the scout vehicle. I'm about ten minutes ahead of our convoy. They should be along in a bit."

"So how did you know we were here?" I asked. "Did you hear my radio transmission?" I knew the Hum-V's antenna was buried; but still, there could have been no other logical explanation for his sudden appearance. At that time, in that place, it would have been a miracle for anyone to just happen by.

"What transmission?" he replied. "We were just passing through here on our way home."

In awe, I collapsed onto the hot sand. My throbbing body could finally rest; my tortured mind, put at ease. Catching the twinkle in the medic's saintly eyes, I believed every word he said. With all my heart, I trusted him.

Sergeant Jason Matthews, the medic, called for a chopper, and then worked feverishly. I was strapped to a long-board, while my pants and shoulder holster were completely cut off of me. My arm was splinted and my neck placed in a bulky brace. An I.V. was administered and through it all, I slipped in-and-out of the real world.

Before long, the medi-vac chopper flew in for the pick-up. After covering me from head-to-toe with a warm foil wrap, Sergeant Matthews placed his entire upper body over my face, shielding me from the blowing sand. The incoming chopper kicked up a mountain of the powder with its giant blades. Touching down, the airborne ambulance's motor was cut down to a high-pitched whine. It was the most welcomed screech I ever heard. Four men lifted up the canvas litter and at a sprint, I was rushed into the helicopter. Looking back at Matthews, I yelled, "Thank you," though there was no way he could have ever heard me. The chopper was too loud.

With a look of urgency, though, Matthews ran over. He grabbed my hand and placed something into the palm. With a wonderful smile, he threw a thumbs-up and was gone.

I opened my hand. It was my gold wedding ban, slightly deformed, but shining brightly. Goose bumps raced over my body. It was too much to be for real. But it was true. I lived through it. I slid the ring back onto my finger and the chopper took to the air.

NOAH KNOWS
BY
BILL MONKS

Chichi was to be placed in a U.N. Trusteeship and the island was to be uninhabited for the next twenty years. Our orders of departure contained the strange request that all livestock on Chichi were to return with us.

NOAH KNOWS
By
Bill Monks

Non-Fiction

The occupation of Chichi Jima after WW II had come to a close; we were finally ordered to return to Guam. We had sent all Japanese troops back to their mainland, all except the prisoners. Chichi was to be placed in a U.N. Trusteeship and the island was to be uninhabited for the next twenty years. Our orders of departure contained the strange request that all livestock on Chichi were to return with us.

The livestock consisted of 19 horses; numerous pigs, goats, chickens, dogs and one monkey named Hojo. Hojo was a member of Charlie Co. He had joined Charlie during the Bougainville campaign. The Colonel had been using the horses found on the Island to whip some of the farm boys into the first and last Marine Corps cavalry outfit. Being a gentleman from Virginia he knew his horses and something about cavalry drills.

The vessel we were to return on was small. The ship was an LST (Landing Ship Tank) mainly used during the war as a landing craft for troops and armor. The ship was 300 ft. in length with a beam of 50 ft. and a crew of 110. It was 1,625 tons with a flat bottom. The most striking characteristic was the large doors that made up its bow. When the craft ran up on the beach these huge doors would open, then like a large tongue, a ramp would come out of the open mouth. Tanks and troops would then spew out onto the beach. I give you all these details because in the following yarn the ship is the main character.

We loaded our strange cargo into the hold, and made them as comfortable as we could among the trucks, Jeeps and the rest of our supplies. The situation did not look too promising for our four legged sailors. We constructed a wooden shack on the main deck to act as a brig for our Japanese prisoners. These men were being taken back to Guam to stand trial for war crimes.

After a day out at sea, the smell of the animals permeated the ship. We were sailing in a dirty barn. It was painful trying to sleep, between the grunting of the pigs, the barking of the dogs, the baa of the goats and the neighing of the horses. We had a regular Spike Jones band below deck. Chickens were starting to wander around the deck.

The second night out, the ship started taking a beating from a heavy sea. We received the word that a typhoon was about to bear down on us and to secure everything. How do you secure a zoo?

A sailor told me that prior to the ship's arrival at Chichi they had lost their regular Captain, who had been transferred to another ship. An inexperienced Executor Officer was now the Acting Captain and the crew did not trust him. The executive was about to get his baptism of fire. Within a couple of hours, the wind had increased in force to 70 mph. I recently consulted the U.S. Weather Bureau for the WD SP of that typhoon in that longitude & latitude during late March, 1946. They sent me a computer printout, which read, 045, 070, 070, 100, 085, 080, 090, 090. As any old swabbie would tell you, that was a blow and a half.

The ship was being tossed and battered in an honest to God typhoon. I stood out on the deck to watch the magnitude and power of the seas. I could actually see the ship bending amidships. The deck plates were continuously crying out in pain. A sailor reassured me that the ship was made to buckle amidships so that it wouldn't snap in half. I felt like crying along with the plates. The ship tipped more then rolled because of its flat bottom, on a good tip you could look UP at the sea. The decks were constantly awash.

WHOOSH! The brig we made for our prisoners went bottom up and blew over the side, leaving the Japanese still on the deck. We ushered them below deck. Our intentions were to hang them not drown them. They must have had some fun in that shack while the ship pitched.

We were to be in the typhoon for several days. We were notified that the port on Guam was closed and to ride out the storm as best we could. I had been in rough weather before but nothing like this. The bow would ride high into the air and then come crashing down to bury itself in the sea. Prior to the storm a sailor had informed me that the doors were damaged and had been jury-rigged to stay closed. I prayed they would.

The huge seas controlled our course. The ship appeared helpless, as the helmsman's metal was being tested, trying to keep the bow into waves in order to keep the ship from broaching. As we left Guam to our stern, the storm increased in velocity. It looked as if we were going to be blown as far south as Truk, in the Caroline Islands. Our brother Regiment, the 21st Marines who were stationed there might be in for a surprise.

I was scared stiff. I wished that I hadn't heard about the doors or the Executive. I always hated a rough sea, but this was like being in a blender.

As you would expect our sailors in the hold were taking heavy casualties. A lot of the poor animals, including several horses had died early on. The dead horses had bloated. The ship reeked from the smell of the dead and the waste of those still alive. This pungent aroma and the ferocity of the storm called for an iron stomach.

All day long the carcass of the horse followed in our wake. Was the mangled equine stalking us? It was positively eerie, was it horse or albatross? A blanket of gloom covered the ship.

I thought of the lines of Coleridge:

And having once turned round, walks on,
And turns no more his head;
Because he knows a frightful fiend
Doth close behind him tread.

The following morning our spirits rose as we finally escaped the storm and headed back to Guam, our pursuer had sunk beneath the waves. As we entered the harbor we breathed a sigh of relief, but it was much too soon.

We were out at sea far longer then we had expected and therefore had to ration our chow and fresh water, not that anybody had an appetite. Marines and Sailors alike would just lie in their sacks with their head in their helmets, The helmets were strapped to the edge of the sacks and at night, as the ship tipped, you would hear the splashing on the deck, as the helmets runneth over.

Some Marines volunteered to go into the hold and hoist out the dead horse carcasses through the main hatch. We all watched as the first horse, hog-tied went out of the hold. The horse was bloated to twice its normal size and swinging like a pendulum. Just as the carcass was about to clear the hold, it broke in half, deluging the working party below, with horse. The audience fell on the deck laughing. Due to a shortage of volunteers that work detail was canceled.

The Executive was about to dock a ship for the first time. If there is any sort of cross wind, combined with the loss of headway, docking can be a very difficult task for any seaman.

As we bore in, the Marines on board were lining the rail checking out the ships in the harbor. We appeared to be closing on a beautiful yacht, the "Lonely Lady," that was tied up to the pier. The sailors, pointing out its flag, told us it belonged to the Commodore of the Island. The yacht was J.P. Morgan class. It was a luxurious showpiece made of wood; its polished brass and varnished deck glistened in the sun. The only person on deck was a young officer, waving to us in a friendly manner, a very cool character. This guy seemed real smug; he knew he had it made. He looked like Ensign Pulver from that play Mr. Roberts, a ninety-day wonder, in new, neatly pressed khaki. His demeanor quickly changed to panic as he realized we had lost headway and were being blown into his side. He started making signs with his hands as if to push us off. It was now obvious we were about to mash the Lonely Lady against the dock. The guy on the yacht deck had by now completely lost it. He was springing into the air, waving his arms and screaming foul language. We came along broadside and tucked the Lonely Lady into the side of the pier.

The Marines were howling with laughter as we watched the polished planks pop and spring into the air. We kissed her, un-puckered and impolitely continued on our way. We had done extensive damage.

143

We never exchanged a word with the maniac; he was not making any sense. This poor guy was in deep trouble with the Commodore. (Officer of the Deck, what deck?) As we proceeded deeper into the harbor, the sailors were cursing the Executive, and the Marine laughter could not be contained.

We are now heading for a docking space between two other LSTs, who have their doors open on to the beach. Sitting ducks! There is about a thirty-yard space between them.

I figure by now every ship in the harbor had their glasses trained on us and we didn't let them down. The docking operation looked to us as easy as parking a car. I'm sure it appeared that way to the Executive. As we approached the gap between the two ships, we slowed our forward motion and again we lost headway. The crosswind caught our bow, crashing us into the stern of the LST on our starboard side. As we back off, we proceed to cream the other ship on our port side with our stern.

We are on the verge of being wedged between them. Nobody has the heart to laugh anymore; by now the Marines are bonded to our ship and we are sharing our shipmate's embarrassment. We can no longer even look.

Finally the three crews fight us free and we eventually dock between the ships. Our sailors want to take the ship back out to sea and go down with it. They all agree that it would not be wise to take shore leave. The other two crews are complaining about a horrible smell.

We no longer notice it; we have become the smell. Now comes the piece de resistance. When the ship is made snug to the beach, the Exec gives the order, "Open the bow doors." Sure enough with all the eyes of Guam staring at us, out of the mouth of our ship comes one hell of a bad breath, followed by the survivors of the typhoon: sick chickens, thin pigs, smelly goats, wild dogs, and a bunch of lame horses. Looking into the hold one can see a bloated horse has commandeered the Col.'s Jeep.

Hojo had been quartered with us, and was in the pink.

I want to know how the heck the Executive got us through that typhoon. I never saw the man. He is now probably living out in Kansas, far from the briny deep.

Next day the headline of the Guam Daily read:
NOAH'S ARK LANDS ON GUAM

THE PROCEDURE
By
Griffin T. Garnett

Griffin T. Garnett was born August 15, 1914 in Washington, D.C. Garnett received his BA from the University of Richmond in June 1936. He then moved to Washington, D.C., attended evening classes at the National University Law School, now a part of George Washington University Law School, and attained his LLB in 1940.

Garnett married Harriet Waddy Brooke of Washington, D.C. in September of 1938. They have two grown sons, one in the law practice with Griffin, and another who is a civilian industrial engineer with the U.S. Navy. Griffin also has three grandsons.

In 1940, Griffin opened his law practice in Arlington. His legal career was interrupted during WWII by his two-and-a-half year stint in the U.S. Navy. While in service, he saw active duty in the S.W. Pacific, serving first as executive officer and later as commanding officer of two landing ships. He left active duty, as a Senior Lieutenant, in 1946, and resumed his law practice.

Griffin's interest in Journalism and creative writing stretches back over many years. He was, during his college days, a freelance writer for the Richmond News Leader. At college, he co-wrote, directed and produced two original musical revues. While at law school, he was, for a period of years, a five-day-per-week statistical columnist for the Washington Times Herald. During his legal career, he originated, co-wrote, directed and produced the Arlington County Bar Association's annual satire. More recently, several of Griffin's creative writings, *Tales from Orchard Point*, have been published in *Pleasant Living*, a Virginia regional magazine. *The Sandscrapers* is the first published novel by the author, followed by *Taboo Avenged*. Visit Griffin at: **http://www.thesandscrapers.com**.

FOREWORD

This is an excerpt from my WWII adventure romance novel, *The Sandscrapers*. For purposes of this anthology, I have entitled this episode "The Procedure." The event takes place on LSM (Landing Ship Medium 460.5 (fictionally numbered)). The ship, a flat-bottomed, ocean-going assault landing ship, was 203 feet in length with a 33-foot beam, a 2.5-foot draft forward and about 5.5-foot draft aft when empty. It had a crew of 5 officers, 13 petty officers and 37 seamen, 1st and 2nd class.

After 18 days at sea unescorted, it had reached a lagoon at Bora Bora Island, one of the French Society Islands in the South Pacific and was awaiting its first refueling. The skipper is "Larry Stapleton;" the executive officer is "Greg Morgan;" the engineering officer is "Norman Chesleski;" the communications officer is "Vernon Young;" and the supply officer is "Jack Yarboro." "Eugene William Foyle" is the pharmacist's mate 2nd class and the only medical officer on board. The episode reported was then recommended by the medical services of the armed forces, but not usually undertaken by a pharmacist's mate 2nd class.

THE PROCEDURE
By
Griffin T. Garnett

Fiction

Greg reported on board at 1600 hours. The ladder guard advised him that the skipper was ashore with the base commander. The exec sensed a strange atmosphere on the ship, as soon as he set foot on the deck. Some off-duty members of the crew were lolling in the well deck at the stern of the ship. They were enjoying quiet convulsions of laughter as they exchanged subdued comments. On the well deck near the bow were five of the crew, Jimmy Wharton, a gunner's mate, Jim Howard, one of the steward's mates, Dave Halloran, a seamen first class, Frank Williams, a second class machinist's mate, along with Abraham Armstrong, the second cook on board. They looked ill, scowling and whispering to each other. All were sitting on low stools, bent over as if in real pain. Greg had no idea what was happening. As he descended the wardroom ladder, he saw Chesleski, Young, and Yarboro seated at the wardroom table. They were convulsed with laughter.

"What the hell gives?" he inquired.

Gasping for breath, the engineering officer was finally able to say, "We have had a mass circumcision aboard today."

"What?"

"You heard me, we have had a mass circumcision aboard today."

"Just what in the name of God are you talking about?"

Chesleski chuckled a couple more times, then reported: "For days, Foyle has been extolling the merits of circumcision to members of the crew, particularly since Walpole, one of the engineering gang, got the clap in Panama. Yesterday, when Foyle went ashore, he met the base pharmacist's mate. That medical attendant has enough supplies left over from the departed MASH unit to serve the pharmacy needs of a battlewagon. Foyle was able to completely refill his medical chest. So, last night when the off-duty crew returned from liberty, he told everyone who would listen how the ship was in very still waters, and that now was the time for all aboard who wanted to be circumcised, to let him know.

"Somehow he conned Seaman First Class Ben Israel, to be his chief salesman and aide in the procedures. Ben advised the men that circumcision was a piece of cake, no pain, and no trouble at all. What he didn't tell them was that he was eight days old when it happened to him, and he didn't remember a damned thing about the procedure. Anyway, the holy five, now on the well deck at the bow of the ship, bought Foyle and Ben's story. Foyle set up his operating table shortly after you and the skipper left ship this morning, and the procedures commenced. Ben was his assistant. He no sooner saw Foyle inject Novocain into the pecker of the gunner's mate when he passed out cold. Israel hit his head on the edge of the table as he fell to the floor. Foyle had to stop the proceedings, revive Israel, and put a Band-aid on the guy's head before he could continue.

"Doc did all five of them within three hours. The circumcised five were fine until the local anesthetic wore off. Right now each of them is ready to kill our 'peckerologist.' Several members of the crew have offered to loan the pecker-peeled five their respective collections of porno magazines. Gunner Wharton has threatened to kill each and every kidding smart alec aboard as soon as his stitches heal. They can barely move.

"Ben Israel has offered to hold the Jewish celebration of circumcision. That's what the crew at the stern of the ship are laughing about. I know we shouldn't be making fun of the episode, and it's a darn good thing we are not putting to sea tomorrow.

"The three of us have read the riot act to Foyle. We have told him he should never have done it, that he is not qualified to perform such procedures and before any such attempt, he should have gotten permission from the skipper. I'm sure that the skipper would never have permitted the surgery. God, Foyle did five of them in three hours."

Greg smiled at his brother officers who were still guffawing over the morning's episode on the ship. "You better let me break this story to Larry when he comes aboard. He isn't going to think it was so damned funny," said Greg.

The junior officers sobered immediately.

"What's the problem?" asked Yarboro.

"Man, do you know what trouble Larry and Foyle could be in if any of those men get an infection resulting from Foyle's procedures?"

"I never thought about that," replied Ensign Young. "But, you are right, and it happened on my watch. I could be in trouble too. Holy Christmas, what a mess that would be."

Chesleski was still tickled by the happenings of the morning. With a sly grin, he quipped, "Just a matter of who has who by the pecker?"

"Shut up you Lithuanian imp," shot back Greg. Serious as the happening was, the exec couldn't help but see the humorous side of the morning's pecker peeling.

Before the foursome could have any further discussion on the matter, their skipper came sliding down the ladder to the wardroom. Without directly addressing any one of the officers seated at the wardroom table, he commented, as he dropped into his seat at the head of the table, "I had the oddest feeling upon boarding the ship. Has something weird taken place on this bucket?" He looked at the faces of the three junior officers who were staring at him. He couldn't tell whether they were holding back tears of laughter or fear. Now he was sure that something had happened. "What the hell are you guys keeping from me?" he shot at them.

Greg broke the silence with the remarks, just as he had first heard them. "There's been a mass circumcision aboard this morning."

"What?"

Greg then related the morning's events as previously told to him. Larry couldn't help but let out a couple of muffled belly laughs. Then his face turned a livid red as he realized the possible serious ramifications of the pharmacist mate's procedures.

"Young, get that crazy, knife-wielding idiot down here right now."

"Yes, Sir," replied the communications officer and he was off like a shot in search of Foyle. Chesleski, still grinning, quietly disappeared up the wardroom ladder.

Greg sat silently eyeing his boss. He knew Larry was at a boiling point, but he also knew that unless Larry's pop-off valve was released before Foyle arrived, the skipper might wreck all of the officers' relationship with one of the most valuable men on board. So, choosing his words carefully, he said, "Skipper, those men aboard who let Foyle perform the procedure did so on their own volition. In fact, they asked him to do it. I'll bet any money, he obtained a written consent from each one. He's no fool. He thought he was doing them a favor. Who knows, maybe he was."

"Who asked you?" hissed Larry. "Does that stupid bastard know what possible consequences his actions might have?"

"I doubt it," responded Greg. "I would first approach him from that angle before you chew his ass out."

"I didn't ask you how I should conduct myself with my pharmacist's mate," seethed Larry.

"I know you didn't. I don't even offer a suggestion. All I want you to do is let off your overflow valve before a respected member of your crew is unintentionally demeaned by you."

"Oh, shut up, you legal bastard—a good legal bastard, at that," said the skipper—and he guffawed again.

Shortly thereafter a quizzical Foyle came down the ladder to the wardroom. He took one look at the officers seated at the table and knew he was in trouble, trouble which he had anticipated might happen.

Larry didn't ask him to sit down. He merely said, "You can stand at ease." Foyle nervously stood, but not at ease.

"You didn't ask my permission to perform those procedures."

"No, Sir," responded Foyle.

"You knew damned well I would not have permitted it, didn't you?"

"I was afraid you might not."

"Afraid I might not? You know very well I could not and would not have permitted multiple pecker trimming."

"Sir," responded Foyle, "I have been trained to take care of the sick and, God forbid, the wounded on this ship, should it be necessary. I have taken part in many medical procedures far more demanding than pecker trimming. Besides that, long before I joined the Navy, even before college, I had helped my Uncle Thaddeus, a pediatrician, in Worcester, Massachusetts, where I lived. I have witnessed and aided in at least fifty circumcisions. In the winter, when they were scheduled at his office and Grace, my uncle's nurse, didn't show up, he would telephone my mom and ask for me to come help him. I would skip high school and act as his assistant. And, they weren't all newborns either. True, I am not a licensed physician, but according to my uncle and the Navy medical staff under whom I trained, I am very adept with minor procedures. So that you know, I got signed consents from each man. They know I am not a licensed physician. But, they considered the procedure essential to their well-being and they had confidence in me."

Larry, still madder than hell, studied his pharmacist's mate. He couldn't help admire the absolute confidence that radiated from Foyle. "Don't you know the trouble you and I will have if any of those men get an infection?"

"I thought of that before I ever talked to them about the procedure. I assume the sole responsibility for that event, should it occur."

"You may say you assume the sole responsibility. Don't you know that it will also fall on my shoulders?"

"How could it? You knew nothing about the pecker peelings until after I completed the procedures. I'll give you a daily report on the men. In a week's time, they should be better than new. Besides, their present condition keeps five of our most eager cock-hounds from becoming too fascinated with the island girls."

Greg couldn't resist a wry smile at Foyle's last remark.

As a parting shot, Larry queried, "What happened to Israel after he fainted?"

"Israel was a real help. The sight of the injected needle was what made him woozy. He quickly recovered. Whenever I was ready to inject, I just told him to look away. He did, and all went fine. Blood doesn't bother him a bit. He is beginning striker studies for a pharmacist's rating. He'll make a good one. It doesn't take long to get over the sight of injections. I know."

Stapleton was perturbed as to how the scene would finally play out. He realized that there was little he could do to change what had happened. So, he sighed and said, "You are dismissed, Foyle."

Foyle saluted and headed for the ladder.

"It will be your ass and mine if anything adverse happens," lamented the skipper to Foyle.

Halfway up the wardroom ladder, Foyle stopped. He smiled

down over his shoulder at his skipper. "If that happens, I really will be worried."

"Why?" shot back Larry.

"Because, I know how to treat your hemorrhoids, but I haven't much confidence in your treatment of mine." Foyle was up the ladder like a shot, slamming the ladder door behind him.

The officers were convulsed with restrained laughter. When he could catch his breath, Larry turned to Greg, "Some day he'll make one hell of a good physician if he doesn't pull any more fool stunts like this last one. Thanks, Greg, for opening my pop-off valve."

Under the watchful eye of Foyle, the five newly foreskin-trimmed members of the crew healed readily and with no ill effects. In ten days time, the incident was forgotten.

There was one lasting and positive result of the episode. The crew, men and officers, had greatly increased respect for and confidence in the capability of their shipboard medical officer. Foyle never again performed the procedure—while aboard the ship.

(Was the foregoing a true story? The least that can be said is that in "*The Procedure*," Greg Morgan is the alter ego of the author.)

AMERICAN PATRIOTS
BY
BETTE MILLESON JAMES

Bette Milleson James, a niece/sister/cousin of many family veterans, is a Kansas writer and award-winning teacher of English language arts and technology. She served her school district as grant writer and later wrote original poetry and did research on classic writers for artist N.A. Noel's book, I Am Wherever You Are. She also has publication credits in two anthologies, Let Us Not Forget, from iUniverse, and Forget Me Knots...From the Front Porch, published by Obadiah Press. She and her husband raised three children on a wheat, corn, and livestock farm west of Hoxie Kansas, where they still live, and where she writes daily.

American Patriots

It was not uncommon that summer and fall for soldiers to be allowed to go home after boot camp to help plant crops or to harvest summer wheat or fall corn before leaving for Europe. But by the end of the year, all the Gardner military men were gone.

AMERICAN PATRIOTS
By
Bette Milleson James

Non-Fiction

It was the summer of 1917, and in the living room of the big house on the Gardner farm near Traer, Kansas, just off US Highway 83 south of the Nebraska line, the six strapping sons of Jonas and Marietta Gardner sat for a formal portrait. Such an event was rare in the family, for the Gardners had been homesteaders and had earned success through long adherence to a staunch and frugal philosophy. Money was not lightly spent on professional photographers, but on that day Jonas and Marietta knew that very soon, some of their sons would be going to fight in the world war that some believed would end all war. They knew, too, because of their childhood memories of the Civil War, what it really was that their children might face.

The sons gathered proudly, dressed in their best, those who would soon be gone and those who would hold the farm and families at home. Patrick Henry and John Thomas, the eldest two, beyond military age, sat in front of their four standing brothers—Arthur, 24; George Washington, 29; Charles Franklin, 26; and young Jonas Randolph, 21. Of these four, only Charlie, a railroader, would fulfill his essential job at home. George, Arthur, and Randolph would serve the military until the end. In doing so, they carried on traditions of service and patriotism that had begun during the Civil War, when Marietta's mother left her children with friends to serve as a nurse in a field hospital that followed the army from battle to battle for four long years, and had continued in the naming of sons after American patriots.

George was one of the first men in Decatur County to be "called up" and the first of the brothers to go. Basic training for the Kansas soldiers was in Camp Funston, near Junction City. George's sister Lenora saved post cards sent from there to her children in November and December of 1917 and January 1918. The tinted photographs on the postcards are entitled "Target Practice," "Shelter Tent Inspection," "Cleaning Rifles," "Getting Ready for Action," and "Packing Kit." The messages are short and simple, intended for children, revealing no dread of future duties.

Randolph, being called next, followed his brother to Camp Funston, and eventually Arthur too was conscripted. After boot camp, Kansas units, composed mostly of farmers, were routinely released to go home and tend to necessary business before shipping out. George, Arthur, and Randolph returned to Decatur County, each separately and in his own turn, where George sold his cattle (a snapshot shows him in his uniform, proudly seated on his horse near the barn) and all three prepared their affairs for a long absence. It was not uncommon that summer and fall for soldiers to be allowed to go home after boot camp to help plant crops or to harvest summer wheat or fall corn before leaving for Europe. But by the end of the year, all the Gardner military men were gone.

George, who received the Distinguished Service Cross, served in Company F, 353rd Infantry. Arthur's service was with "WAGR 32 Engineers," and Randolph was in "Co A 339 MG BN 88 Div." In was Randolph who suffered the deepest tragedy, for his unit was subjected to the trauma of Germany's infamous mustard gas attacks.

On November 23, 1918, George sent Christmas cards from "Somewhere in France" to members of his family in Kansas and Nebraska. Eventually they were "passed" and signed by the censor, a Capt. John Delany, some postmarked as late as December 14, to begin their long ocean journey to the waiting families. War news, always welcome, came slowly and sporadically at best, and even the few words on a small card were treasured at home.

In the end, all the Gardners made it back to Kansas after the war, but not all of life returned to normal. George, having served both in battle and as a member of the occupation army, sent a postcard ("Compliments of Jewish Welfare Board, United States Army & Navy") assuring his family that "Co. F, Regt. 353" had landed safely on *Leviathan* on May 22, 1919, and that he was going to "some camp here for a few days." On returning to Kansas, George eventually married, raised a family on a small farm near Oberlin, and served for many years as the Oberlin City Constable. Arthur, too, after serving his tour of duty "stateside," returned to Kansas to farm, although he never married.

Randolph was not so fortunate as his brothers and was in a way a casualty of the war, although he did come home. For nearly two years, he struggled for a return to normal life, but was deeply affected by the gassing of the troops, and was ultimately unable to forget the horrors he had experienced. Finally, in 1920, George took his young brother to a veterans' care home in Kansas City, and later the family found it necessary to remove him to the Chiropractic Psychopathic Sanitarium for Disabled Veterans in Davenport, Iowa. A 1929 photograph shows a large group of veterans and nurses on Armistice Day, seated in front of a decorated bus. On top of the bus is a sign reading, "We fought in the World War 'over there' but we are fighting for our health 'over here'." Marietta's beloved youngest son, his father's namesake and the pride of his brothers, spent the rest of his life—33 years—in the sanitarium suffering from the effects of mustard gas and "shell-shock," a casualty of the First World War who was lost forever to his family as surely as if he had died in France.

Thus, the first great war of the twentieth century, like all wars before and since, demanded far more of the combatants than they could have imagined in the innocence of their inexperience. Like all families, this one continued to pay for the hard-won freedoms for many years through pain, sorrow, and loss, for those who were touched by the war were touched by it forever. George never forgot the pain of taking his brother away, nor did his children forget seeing that pain and hearing of it. Marietta and Jonas, who had already buried a stillborn infant and a four-year-old daughter, saw their youngest son placed in a living grave, lost to them, and Jonas died within the year. Charlie's son, mindful of family traditions and raised in the midst of them, lived his life's career in the military. Lenora's daughter, like her grandmother before her, served as an army nurse in her own time. Lenora and her sisters saved cards and letters, and we still have them today, testimony to the family's experience.

No matter the surface level of treaties made—and kept or broken—there is a deeper level of events that war cuts through, in the lives of those who die and those they leave behind. It steals more of life than seems possible to those who sit for formal photographs in preparation for the departure, or to those who face the long absence of their loved ones. Families all over America experienced these things, and in every family, even now, there is someone who knows, someone who remembers. Together, those people comprise a national remembrance that goes beyond treaties to the heart of life itself.

A WALK IN THE WOODS
BY
SCOTT PALTER

I have been a game [board and RPG] designer, developer and publisher for three decades as well as running businesses in import/export and retailing. My published fiction so far has been limited to RPG related projects. I have a history degree from Dartmouth and a law degree from Stanford. Although I move frequently I am currently living in Madison, WI with my feline overlord Joshua.

Just lost American soldiers in the midst of a disaster, trying to find someplace to go besides into a POW cage. His butterbars made him senior but how in charge he was had never exactly been put to the test.

A WALK IN THE WOODS
By
Scott Palter

Fiction
Final Sword Productions LLC 2005

Lieutenant Smith was over the crest of the hill before he saw the three of them. The greenhorn, the hillbilly and the Injun were crouched a hundred yards down the glorified cow path arguing. Motioning to the men behind him to take ten, he slid forward on the snowy down-slope to find out what the problem was this time.

"Find us another way". This from the hillbilly, a slim wiry PFC from some hollow halfway to nowhere.

"You does not want another way." This from the greenhorn whose grasp of English seemed flexible at best. The stripes of his coat said corporal but given how oversized it was on the small, olive hued middle-aged man wearing it, it could have been 'borrowed' rank.

"We better want another way. Been down that path of yours. Crosses a real road. Wall to wall Krauts." This from the Injun. He was descended from people that had danced across Arizona and Sonora ahead of two armies. He seemed to find avoiding panzers to be just as easy.

Smith caught it as he slid to a stop and plopped onto his ass from the bad footing. "Talk to me people."

All three looked at him but no one spoke. Took Smith a minute to realize that all three were waiting for him to decide who spoke first. Smith's ninety-day wonderness hadn't rubbed off yet. This collection of strays from four divisions was his first independent command. Fourteen men beside himself, none of who had known each other three days earlier. Smith had stumbled into the greenhorn when it was only a group of four counting the Injun. Just lost American soldiers in the midst of a disaster, trying to find someplace to go besides into a POW cage. His butterbars made him senior but how in charge he was had never exactly been put to the test.

"You first." He pointed to the hillbilly who was the least alien to him of the three. What did a New England college boy like Smith know of Indians and greenhorns were people you saw in the cities but didn't really talk to.

"Big chief and me scouted ahead down the trail he wants us to take. Crosses a big road. Wall to wall krauts. Tigers, halftracks, trucks, marching columns..."

Smith looked at the greenhorn who said, "Yes, we must cross that road. I've kept us to back trails as best I can but the town we wish to go to requires that trail."

157

"Why that town?"

"If your General Ike is sending troops he will send them through that town. Major road junction. There was part of a tank division there before the Germans hit. It is probable he reinforces there. If not we see which of the five roads doesn't have Germans and know which way to go."

"How do you know this track gets us to this town?"

"I worked this area for a few years before coming to America. I know the back trails, the roads, and the towns. It was going on a decade ago but these hills don't change."

"You from around here?"

The greenhorn laughed but there was no humor in it, "Much further east. But it was bad there. Left with some fellow townsmen. No papers or languages. You do what you must. There are always people who need cheap labor, need people who don't see much, don't talk much..."

The hillbilly gave him a look. "So when you were in these hills –"

"The men I worked for here were contrabandist...smugglers. Load trucks. Unload trucks. Drive trucks. Fix trucks. It is work. It is food. It is a way to papers and a seaman's card on a ship to America."

"So you work your way across Europe to get drafted?"

"Draft never finds me. I volunteer day Japs bomb US. It my country now. It is at war. I fight. Same as any of you."

The hillbilly chuckled. "You'll do. At least you don't quite speak the language like a damned Yankee. But that doesn't get us across that road alive."

"People see what they wish. Get American style helmets back in packs. Dust snow over uniforms to hide shape and color. Carry things like work detail. I speak enough German. We get small break in traffic we just walk across."

"Craziest idea I ever heard."

"Who looks at work party? Who looks for enemies walking casually behind officer?"

Smith wasn't sure he was really in charge so the direct statement carried the tone of a hesitant question, "Anyone got a better idea?"

He was met with two frowns but dead silence. "OK. I'm following the greenie. Anyone else doesn't agree split off. No rank here. Just a bunch of guys doing the best they can." The hillbilly thought for a moment and nodded. The Injun seemed more dubious but fell in at the tail of the column after Smith put it to the men and no one wanted to leave.

Forty minutes later the same threesome was in front of the group behind a small rise near the main road. The traffic seemed endless even in the dark. Smith was having second thoughts when a truck blew a tire and pulled off the road. After thirty minutes of commotion the driver and helper abandoned it and walked off into the chaos by the road, leaving a very young man with a rifle to guard the truck. The greenhorn shrugged off his US Army great coat without a word and walked out towards the truck.

The guard called out something and a conversation ensued. Ten minutes later he came trotting back with the guard. Smith watched incredulously as the greenhorn introduced the boy as Karol. Ethnic German from a district near his original home.

"And you brought him back here why?" This from the Indian who was still dubious about everything the greenhorn was doing.

"Boy wants out of the war. He helps us and I promise we send him to prisoner cage back home, let him see cowboys like Hollywood movies. Promised he could meet an Indian. You Indian?"

The Indian's answer wasn't printable but he smiled when he said it.

Hillbilly was half laughing. "Karol. A girl name. How does girl name get us across?"

"Need some help while I patch the tire. Doesn't have to be great. Just hold for few miles." The greenhorn thought for a minute, "Had to translate kilometers into miles, still not used to this mile thing. Three or four miles and we have our turnoff."

Hillbilly was chuckling now. "We gonna steal the truck?"

"Ford truck. We give to British. They give to Ivan. Fritz steals from Ivan. We take back from Fritz. Still Ford truck. Right color. Wehrmacht grey. We pull back into traffic."

Smith kept waiting for something to go wrong but nothing did. From the road they were a work party fixing a vehicle and then piling into the back. The greenhorn even got a German MP to stop the column long enough for them to pull back into the traffic flow. As the truck pulled away he tossed the MP a pack of American cigarettes and got thanks yelled out to the truck's retreating shape.

The tire was a less than perfect fix. It bounced them around but held long enough to reach the turnoff. The hillbilly followed the greenhorn's direction and pulled off onto the trail.

Smith asked, "Now what?"

"We use truck till tire dies or truck dies on trail. Bad ride still better than walk in snow and ice. Twenty-two kilo...no must be American, thirteen miles and we reach town. US lines probably sooner. Parachute men there. One's with big bird on shoulder. Some tanks also. One of you do talking when we cross lines. My accent..."

Hillbilly chuckled again, "Yeah you could pass for a kraut to an outpost that's on edge for line crossers. We can fight beside these airborne guys till somebody sorts things out. What's name of this town?"

"Bastogne".

AN UNCONFLICTED CALL TO DUTY
BY
ROBERT DENSON III

Robert Denson III is the son of an American hero, Robert Denson, who served in World War II. Robert is a husband and also the father of one son, Vincent. Robert lives in Alabama and is the driving force behind Sunpiper Media.

Sgt. Robert Denson
New Guinea, South Pacific

Requested Epitaph of Robert Denson
You Live to Learn and Die to Forget It All. I Am What I Am!

AN UNCONFLICTED CALL TO DUTY
By
Robert Denson III

Non-Fiction

"Don't let them tell you black people didn't fight in World War II, Son," he told me. "When Hitler was destroying Europe and the Japanese were taking over the South Pacific, too many American soldiers were dying. General MacArthur needed men to fight; he didn't care what color they were as long as they fought for the red, white and blue."

My father liked to talk about the unsung soldiers of World War II. He did not distinguish between the soldiers because he thought they were all heroes. Though they were all enlisted into the same U.S. Army, they did not all serve in the same U.S. Army.

"I remember hearing the radio announcement from President Roosevelt on that Sunday. I knew then that America had finally been pushed too far," he said. "But I didn't go sign up to get sent halfway around the world to get shot at."

When I asked my dad why he did not feel the urge to pick up arms and defend his country, with conviction (and a hint of anger), he didn't mix words with me.

"It wasn't my country, son. Things were different when I was your age. You grew up in a time where you were told you had constitutional rights. I grew up in a time when a black man could have a pocket full of money and still could not walk into a restaurant and get something to eat. I had a wife and a three-year old daughter to think about, I didn't have a problem with Germans or the Japanese people. They couldn't have treated me any worse than some so-called Americans did."

I laughed when he told me this. Until the day he died, my father would scoff at a Volkswagen or any Japanese car on the market. He didn't even think the cars should be sold in the United States. So much for his not having a problem with Germans or the Japanese. Needless to say, he did not accept my levity very well, so I wiped the smile off my face and asked him, "So, what did you do?"

"I did what I always did," Dad said. "Until I got drafted, then I did what every other soldier did—I fought."

Though he'd expressed his contempt for the way he was treated in his homeland of Alabama, he stated his call to duty 'matter-of-factly' as if it were a simple choice or not even a choice at all. During his service in World War II, Robert Denson became a non-commissioned officer. Sergeant Denson was proud of his service in the United States Army and his face would often light up when he discussed it.

"I was there in the South Pacific when General MacArthur vowed, 'I will return!'" He told me. Then, with a smile that could brighten the darkest place he said, "And I was there in the Philippines when he returned!"

My father had an uncanny respect for General Douglas MacArthur. He admired the General in his position as Supreme Commander of the Allied Powers. He often bragged about MacArthur wading upon the shore of Leyte. "Soon after that, he fully liberated the Philippines and orchestrated the Japanese surrender." My father felt as if he played an instrumental part of MacArthur's actions: both the failures and successes.

As I continued to hear the wonderful stories about his service, I finally asked him, "So, what was the worst part of your tour of duty?" With this question, his smiled faded quickly. As if I had opened a door and allowed a demon to enter the room, my father dropped his head.

"They make it look glorious on television, Son," he began, "but there is nothing glorious about taking another man's life."

I awaited him to compose himself. After a few minutes, he continued.

"When I was in New Guinea, our captain sent me and another soldier ahead as scouts. He and I moved slowly through the jungle; he on one side of the road and me on the other."

"Did you walk down the road itself?" I asked.

"No. We were looking for an ambush so we crept about fifty yards outside of the road and we radioed back what we saw. The idea was that if there was an ambush set up, we would see it from behind and alert our unit." He explained.

"As we got half way down the road, I came across a very small camp. It looked like it would be big enough for three or four soldiers. I called to my partner and told him to hold tight that there was something I needed to check out. He was supposed to stay on alert."

"As I crept toward the site, I didn't see anything threatening. There was a small tent and a place in front where a fire may have been. As I approached the tent, I heard a strong rustling of the bushes headed in my direction. As I turned to see, there was an Asian man charging towards me with a big knife."

I found myself sitting on the edge of my seat. Although I realized that I would not be alive and breathing if my father had been killed in this story, he told the story with such suspense and emotion and I waited on bated breath.

"I stepped to the side and knocked him down," he said. "I noticed that his knife was a hunting knife and that he did not have a uniform. At that point, I stepped backwards. I yelled to him that I did not want to hurt him, which was stupid because he couldn't understand English." The old man actually chuckled at himself when making that statement. I joined in his humor.

"At that point, I saw a hand come out of the tent and hand him a gun. I stood on ready and screamed at him to put it down. Of course, he still didn't understand me. As he grabbed the gun and pulled it to his shoulder, all I could think of was my three-year-old daughter back at home. It was either him or me and I did not want to go back home in a body bag."

At that point, my Dad fell silent. I sat patiently for a moment and after my patience was fully depleted, I asked him, "So, what happened?"

He looked up at me and said, "It seems that his concern was the same concern as mine."

At this point, I was completely confused. "What do you mean?" I asked.

"I did what I was trained to do, Son," he said with authority. "I was in that jungle to protect my unit and my country and I couldn't do that dead. I did what I was trained to do. I pulled the trigger."

Since I'd never dressed in the uniform of an American soldier, I remained puzzled. I looked to my Dad and said, "You did what you were supposed to do. If you hadn't killed him, he would have killed you and your whole unit would have been in danger. Why are you so upset about that?"

"Because he was not the enemy, Son," He said in disgust. "In that tent were the man's wife and son. He was protecting his family. He probably thought I was there to do something to his wife. He wasn't a soldier; he was a husband and a father and I killed him! He hadn't done anything to my country or me. He died because we could not communicate; because we were different."

Allowing him to wrestle with his disgust, I remained silent for a moment. I could feel the pain and frustration that my father had obviously carried with him for sixty years. I gave his emotions its proper respect but it hurt me deeply to see the pain in his eyes. With a tear in my eye, I said to him, "I'm glad you pulled the trigger."

His head snapped to me. With a frown on his face as if I'd just spat on his shoe, he asked, "What?!"

I gulped and repeated what I said, "I'm glad you pulled the trigger Daddy. Look around you." I reminded. "If you'd not pulled that trigger, I wouldn't be here and neither would my son. Not only am I glad you pulled that trigger, I am proud you pulled that trigger and I thank you. You pulled that trigger for me, Daddy. Thank you."

My father only looked at me. Though we spoke no more about the situation, the looks between our eyes said it all.

My father did not carry this burden much longer. Approximately three months after we had that conversation, he passed away. Since we were at war, the military could not afford to send three soldiers out to grant the twenty-one-gun salute, however, a soldier in full uniform attended and awarded the United States Flag to my mother. My mother requested that the flag be given to the 87 year-old, fallen soldier's only son. I was that son.

I hold that flag dearly and I think of that story every time I see it. It reminds me of how proud I am to be the son of an American soldier and how proud I am of the soldiers that wear that same uniform today. Thank you American Soldier!

In loving memory of
Sgt. Robert Denson
1917 - 2004

You Live to Learn and Die to Forget It All. I Am What I Am!

Printed in the United States
52687LVS00002B/142-177

9 780977 005024